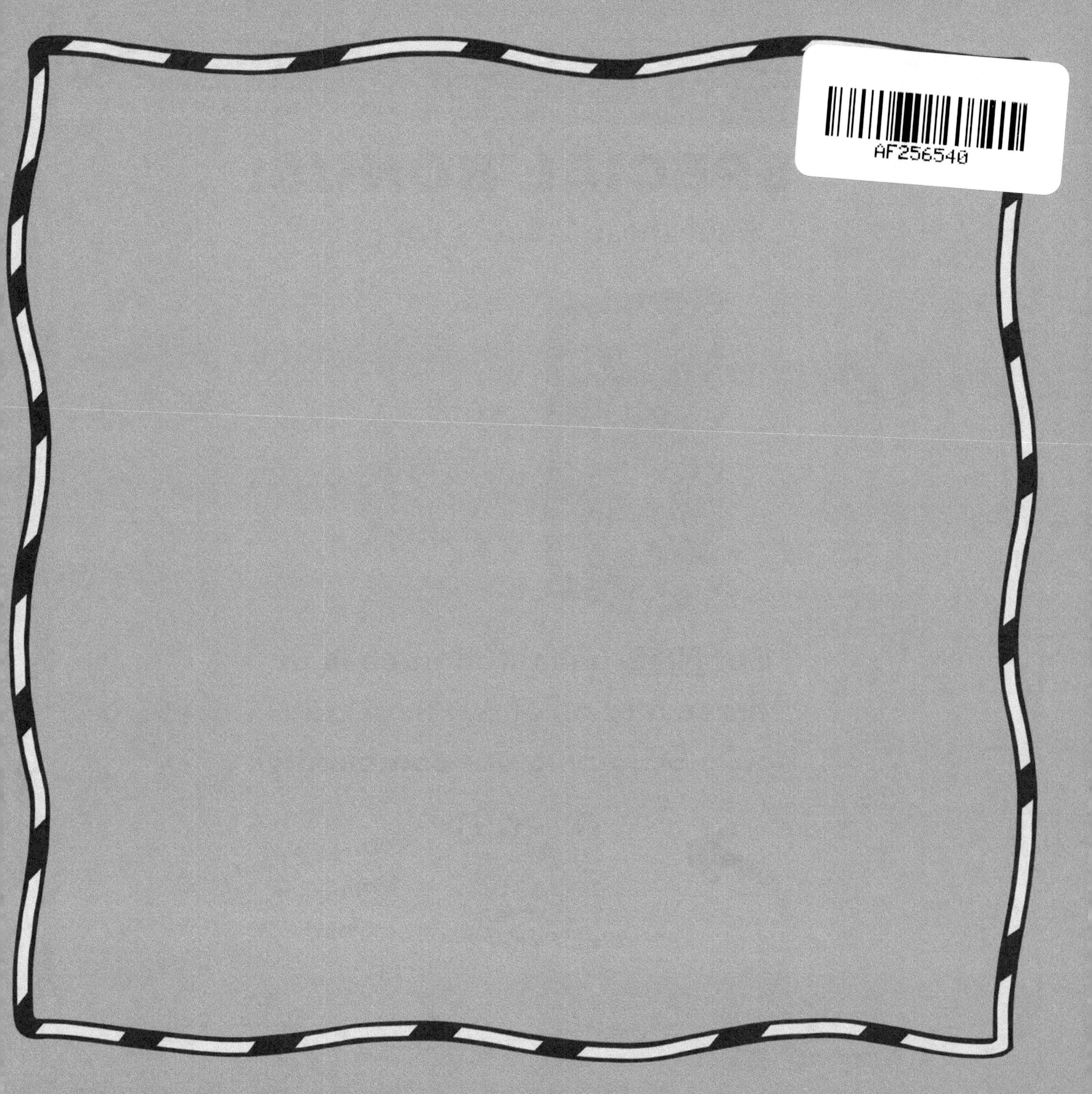

SPECIAL BONUS!

Want These 2 Books For <u>FREE</u>?

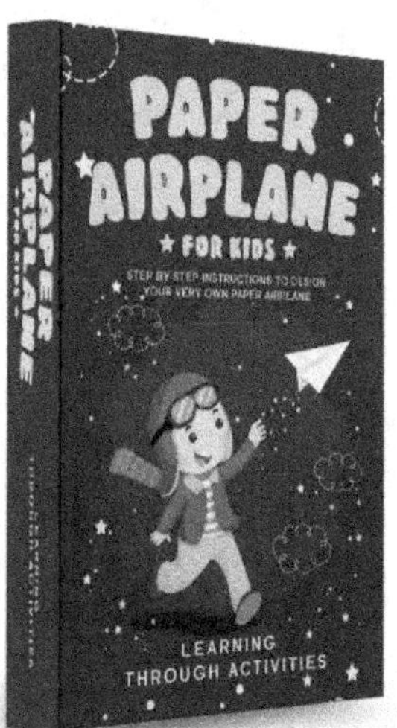

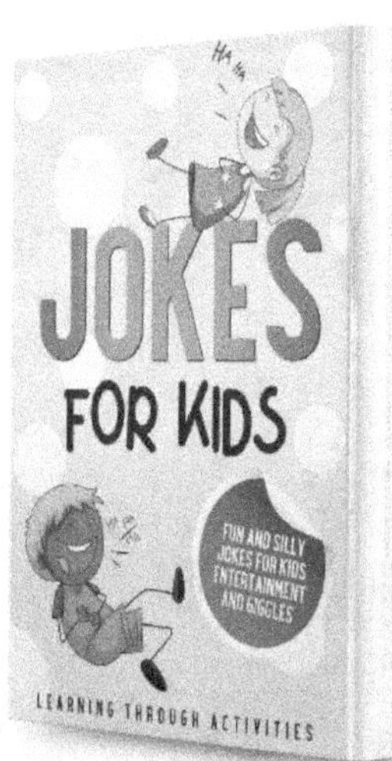

Get **<u>FREE</u>**, unlimited access to these and all of our new kids books by joining our community!

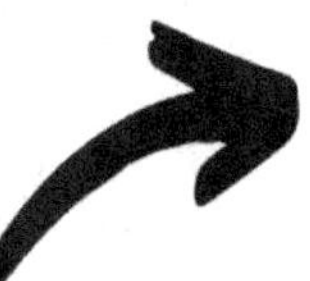

Scan W/ Your Camera To Join!

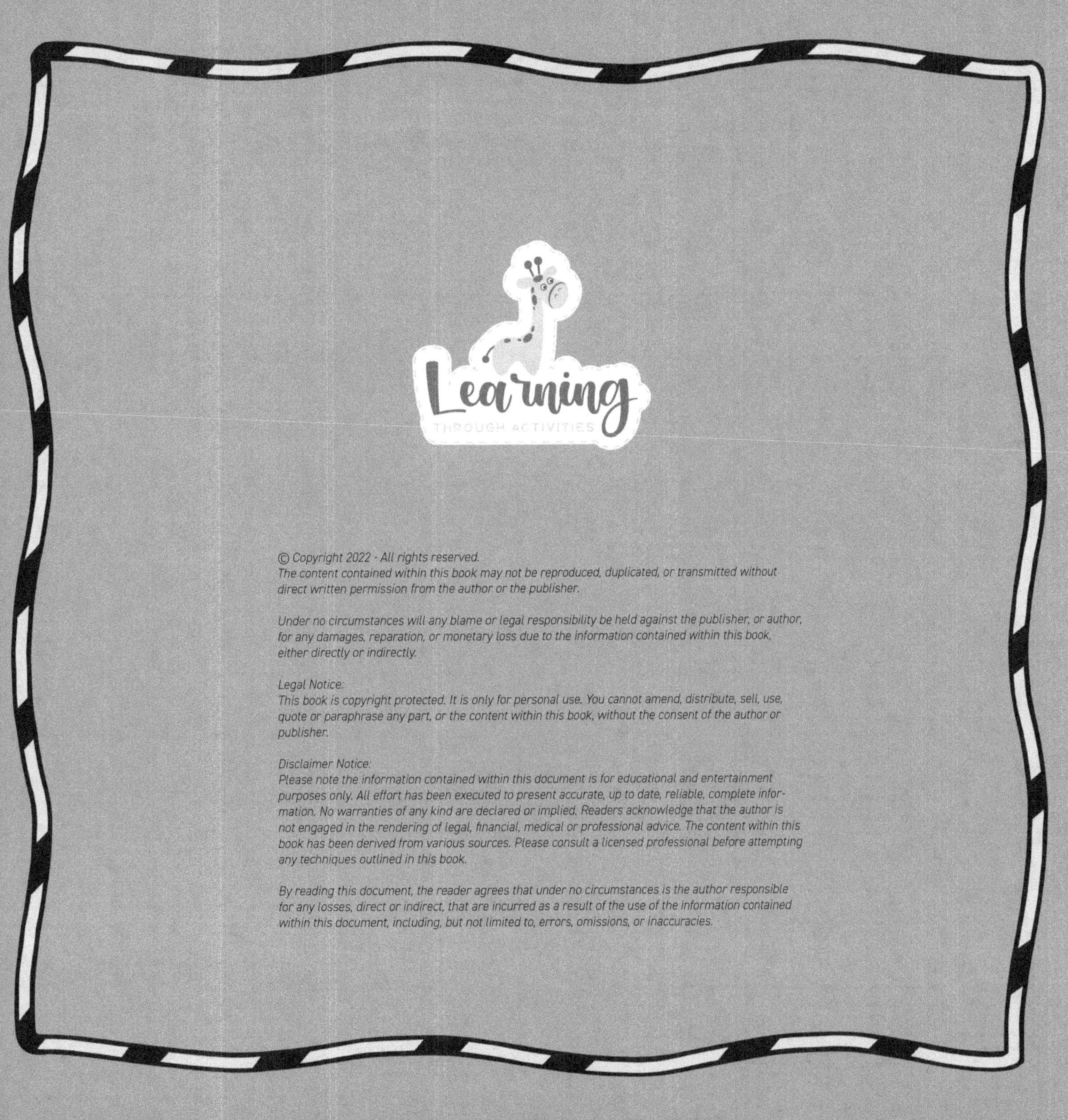

Table of contents

I Spy With My Little Eye
Something Beginning With ...

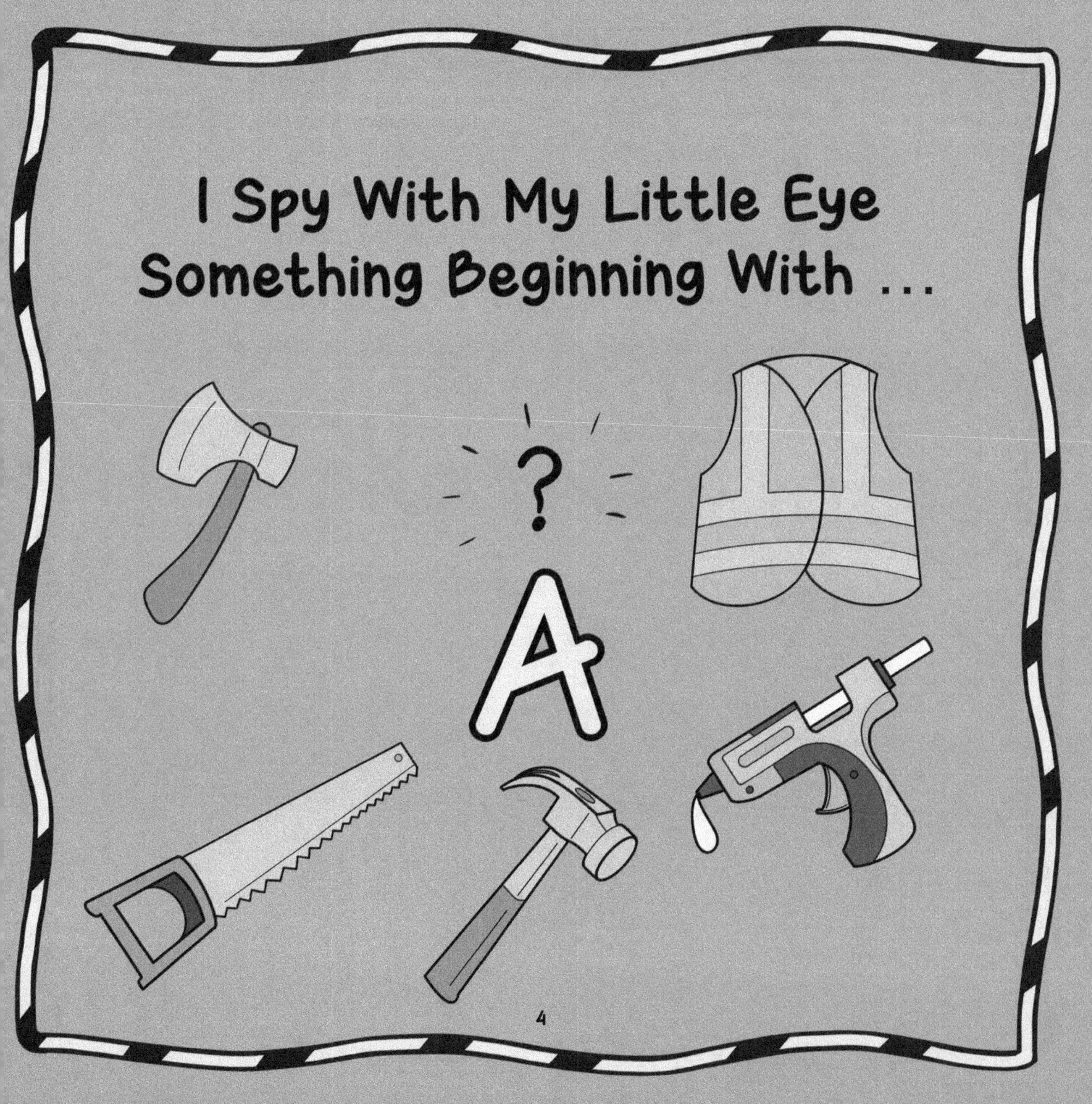

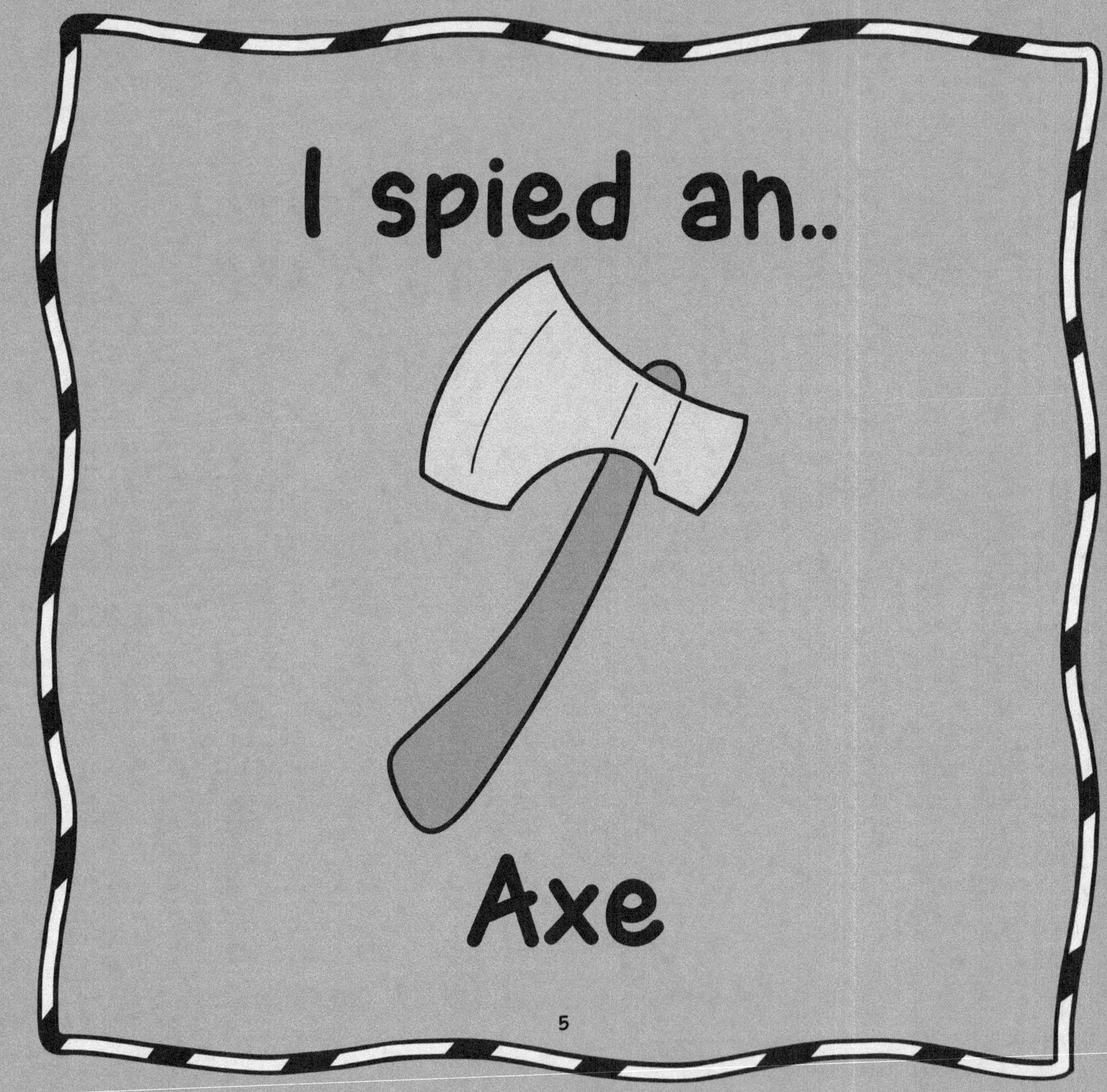
I spied an..
Axe

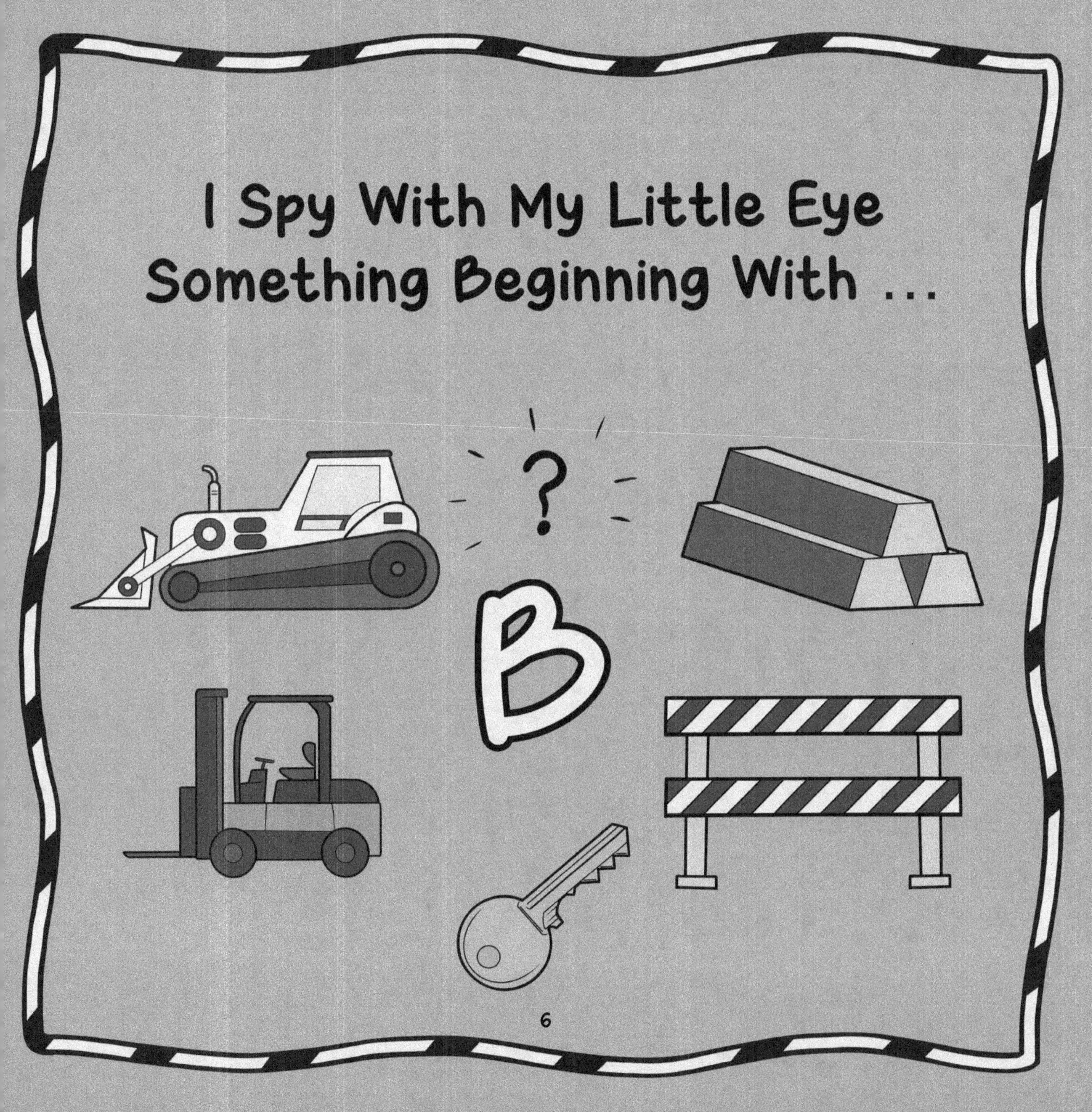

I Spy With My Little Eye
Something Beginning With ...
?
B
6

I spied a..

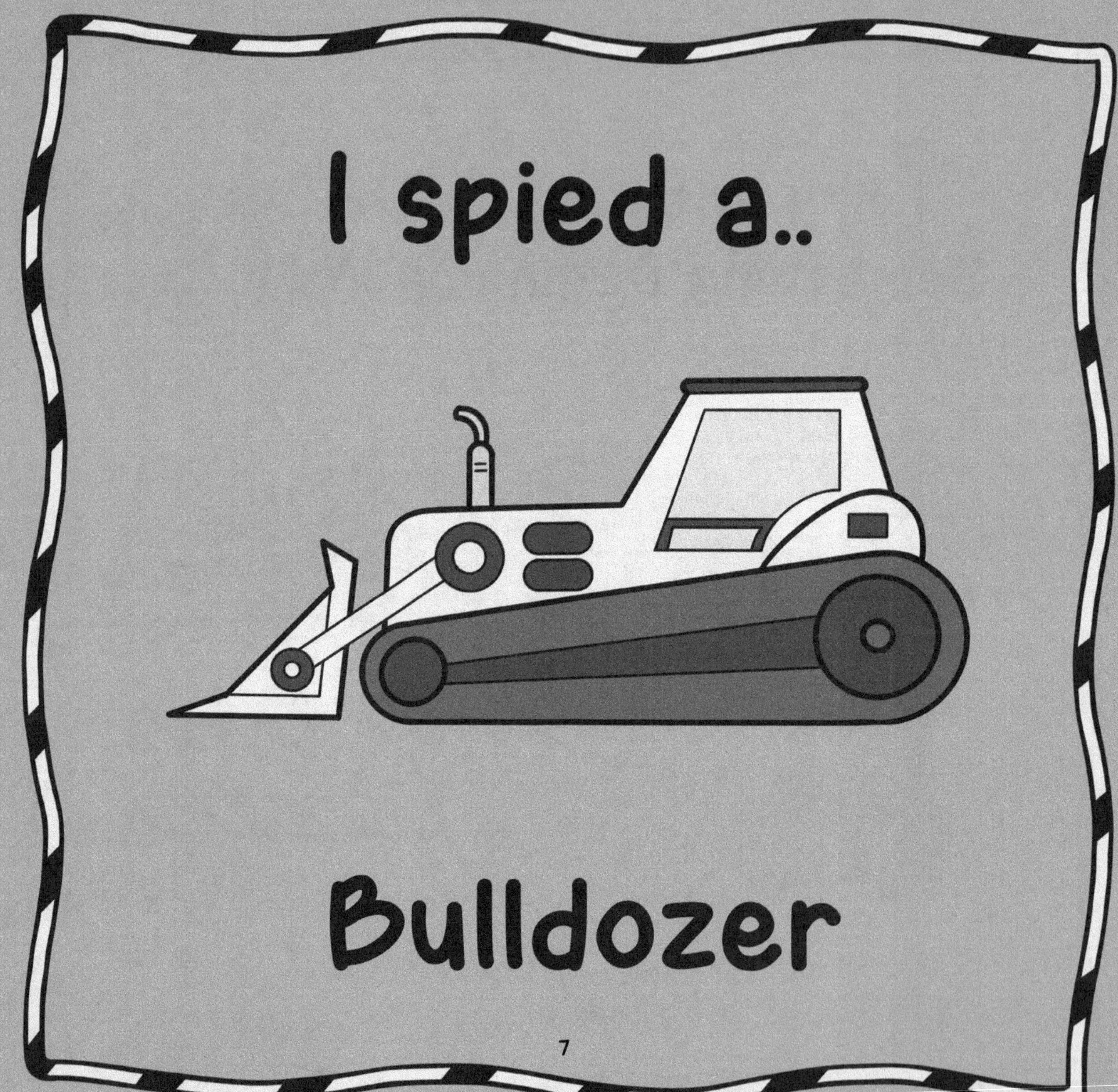

Bulldozer

I Spy With My Little Eye
Something Beginning With ...

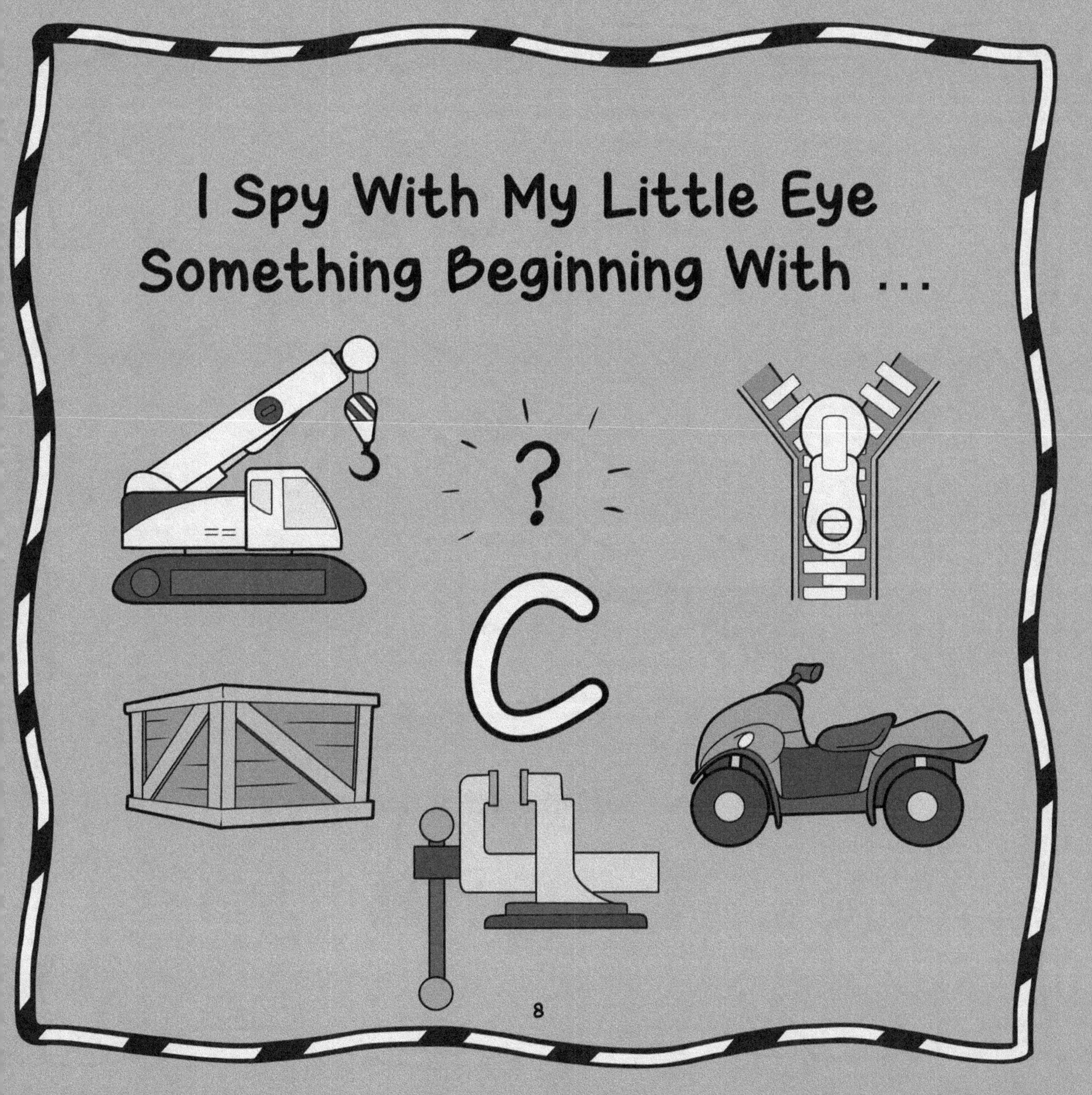

8

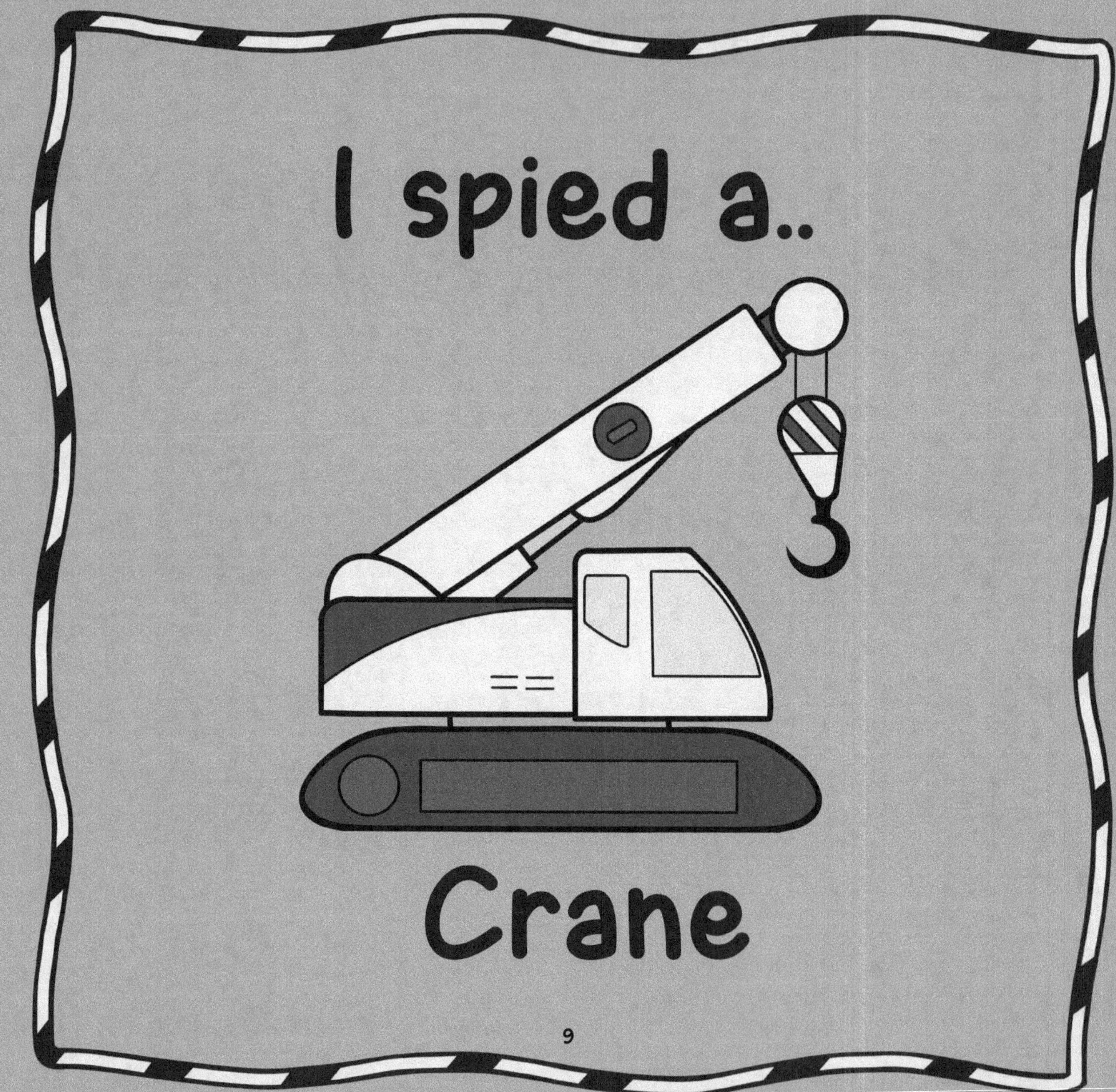

I spied a..
Crane

I Spy With My Little Eye
Something Beginning With ...

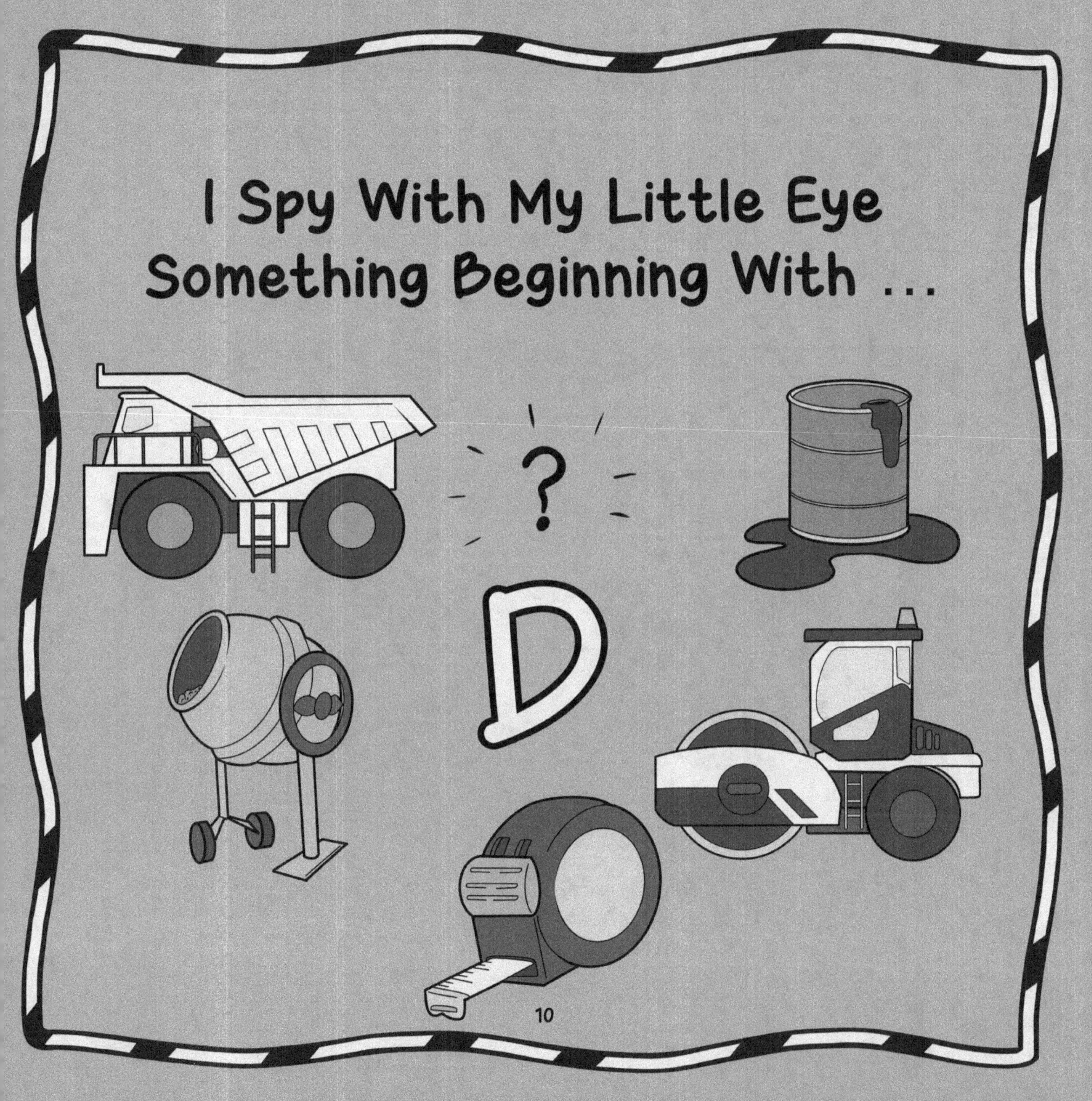

I spied a..

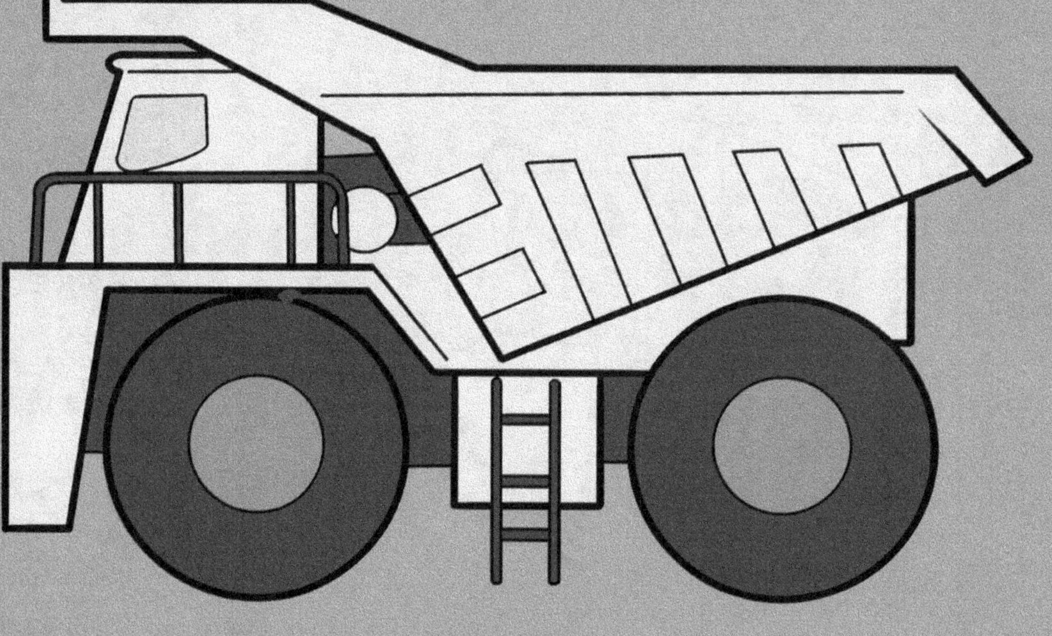

Dump truck

I Spy With My Little Eye Something Beginning With ...

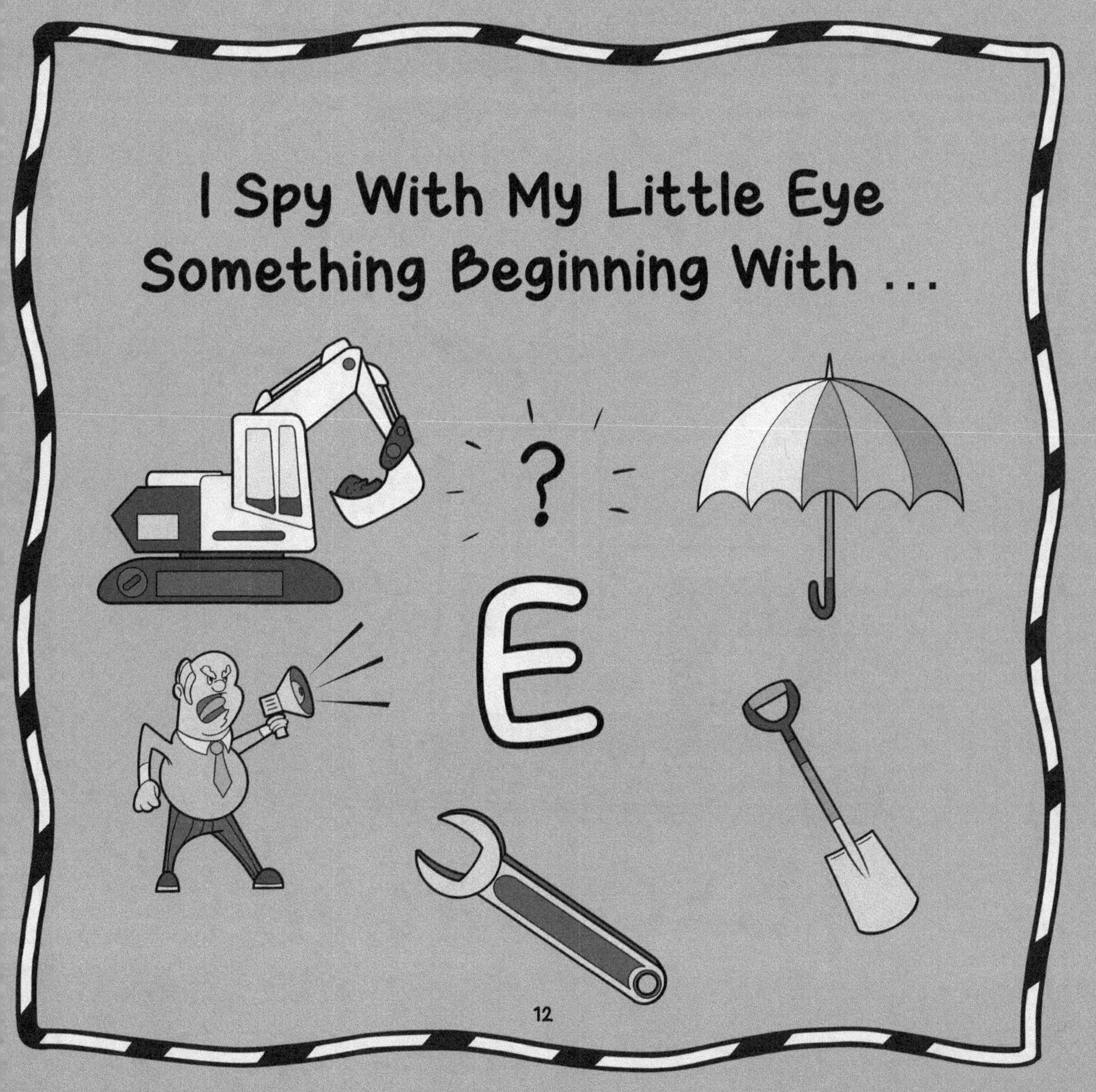

I spied an..

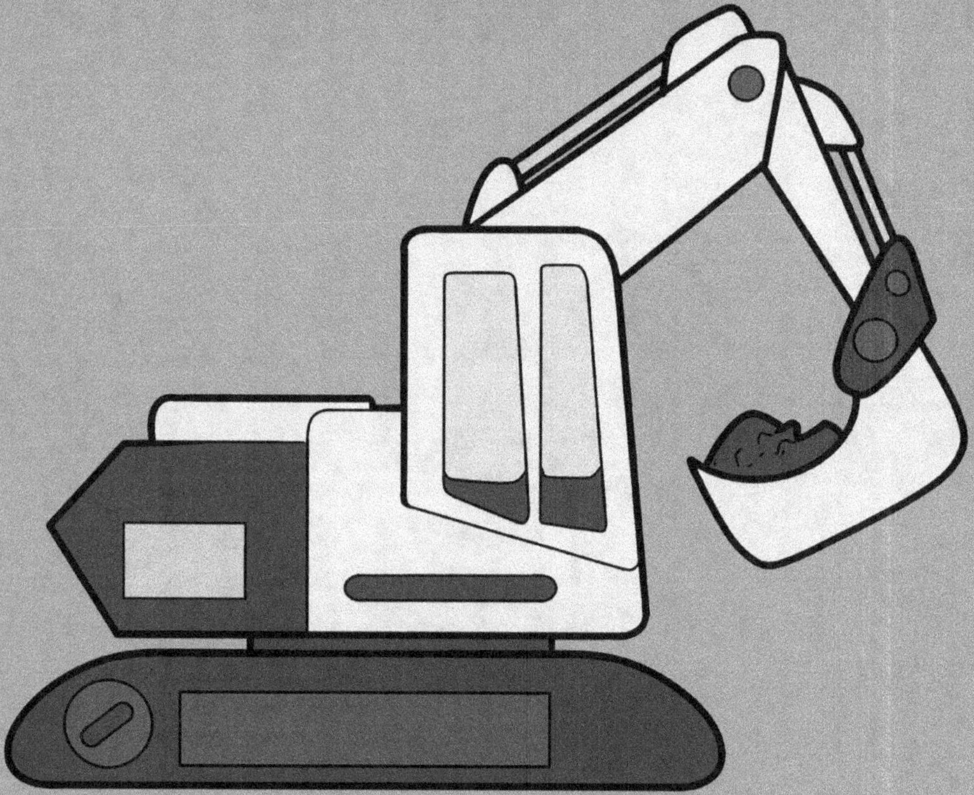

Excavator

I Spy With My Little Eye
Something Beginning With ...

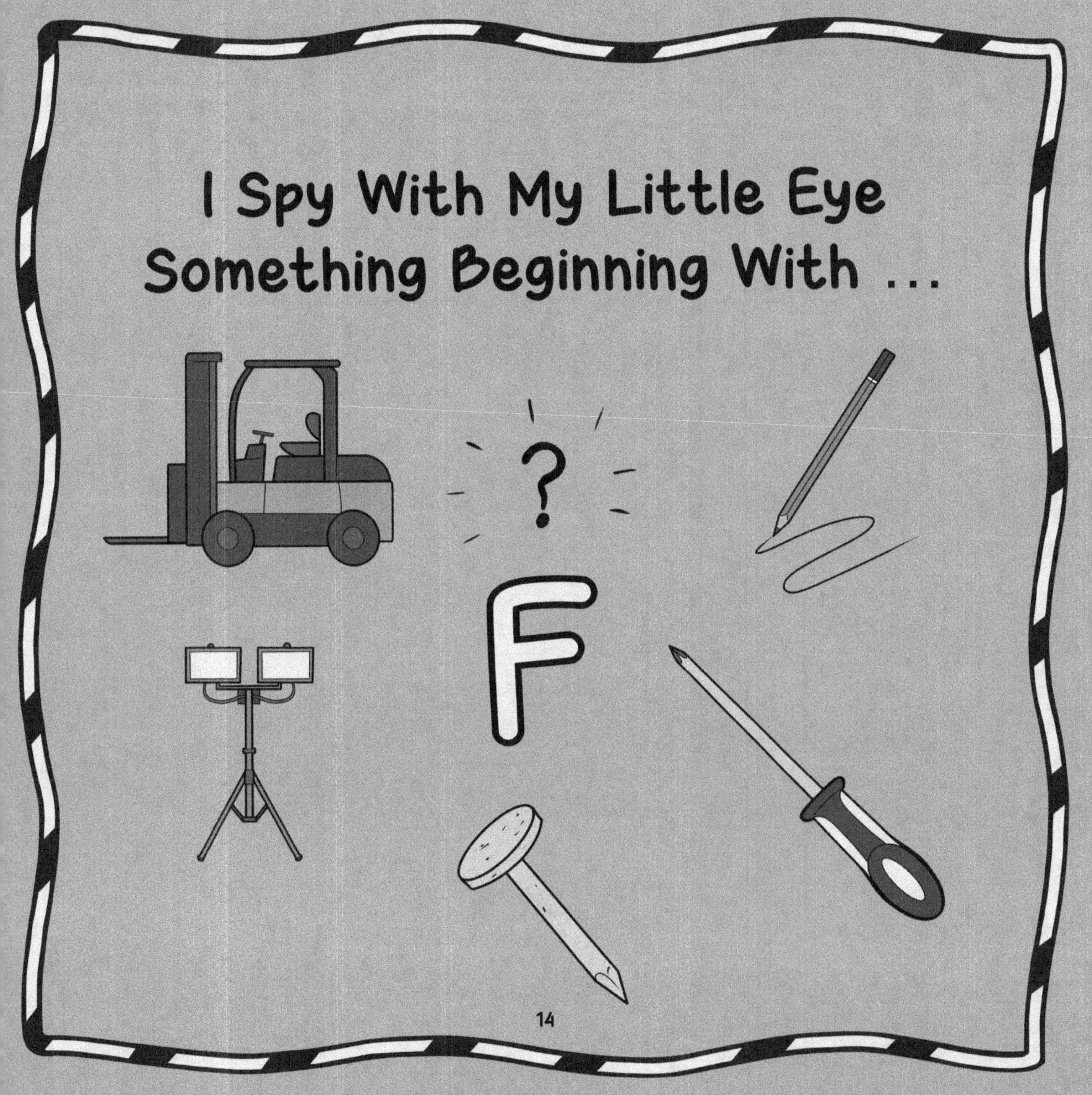

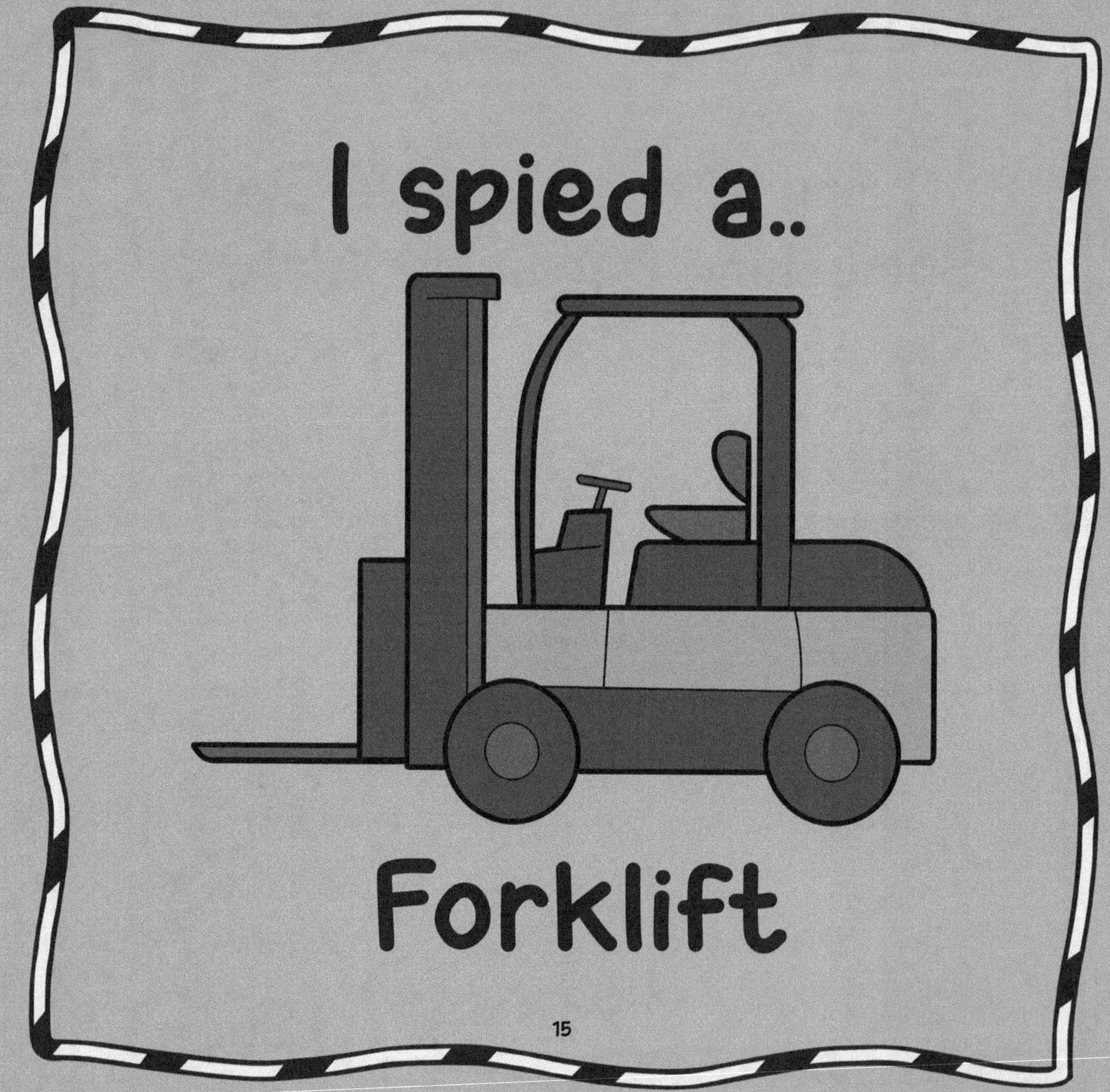

I spied a..
Forklift

I Spy With My Little Eye
Something Beginning With ...

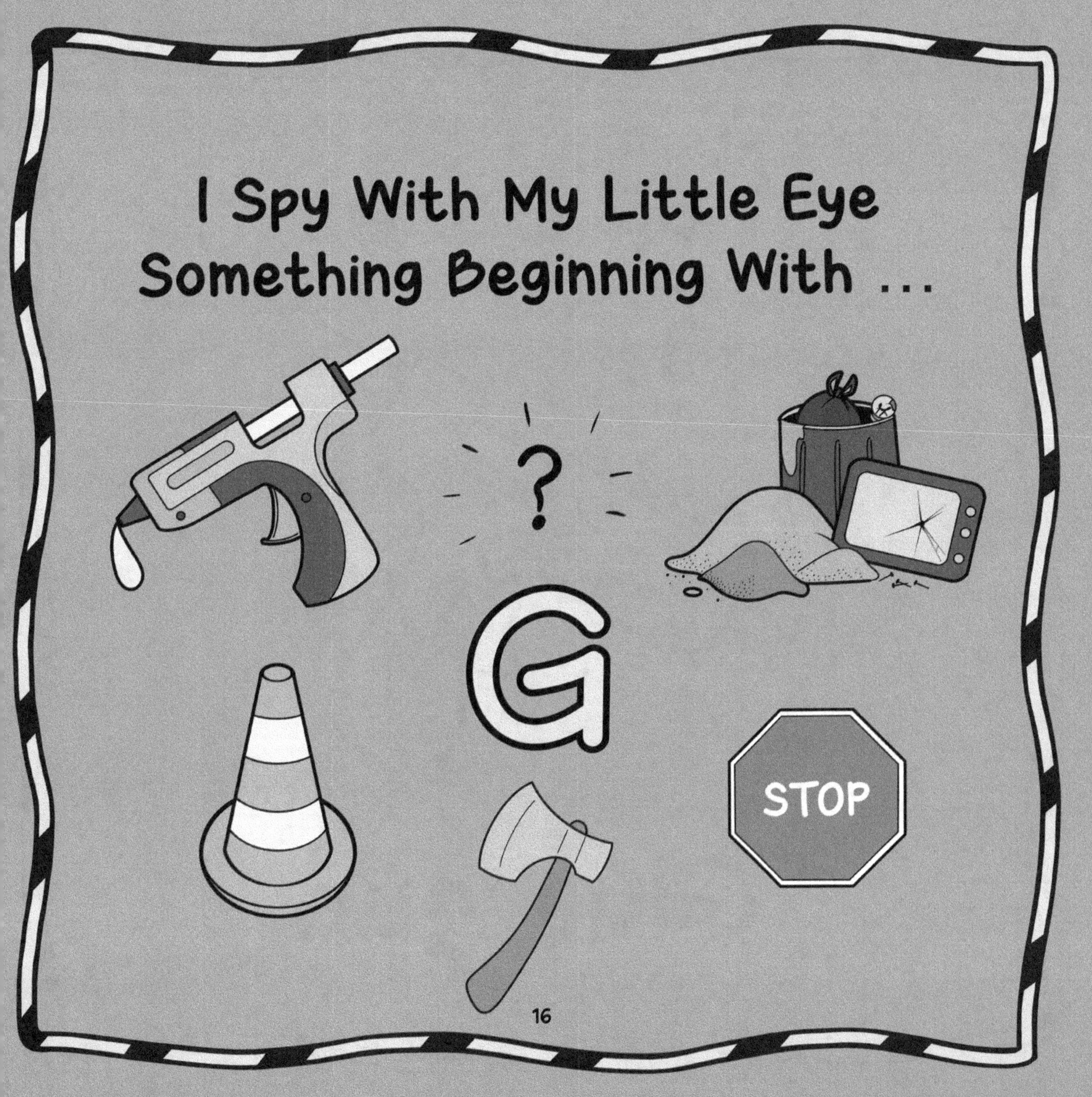

I spied a..

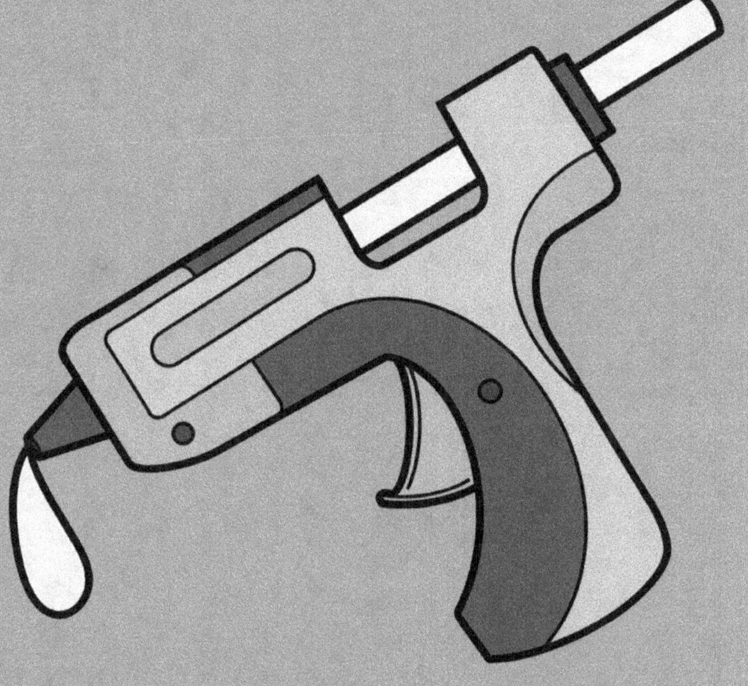

Glue gun

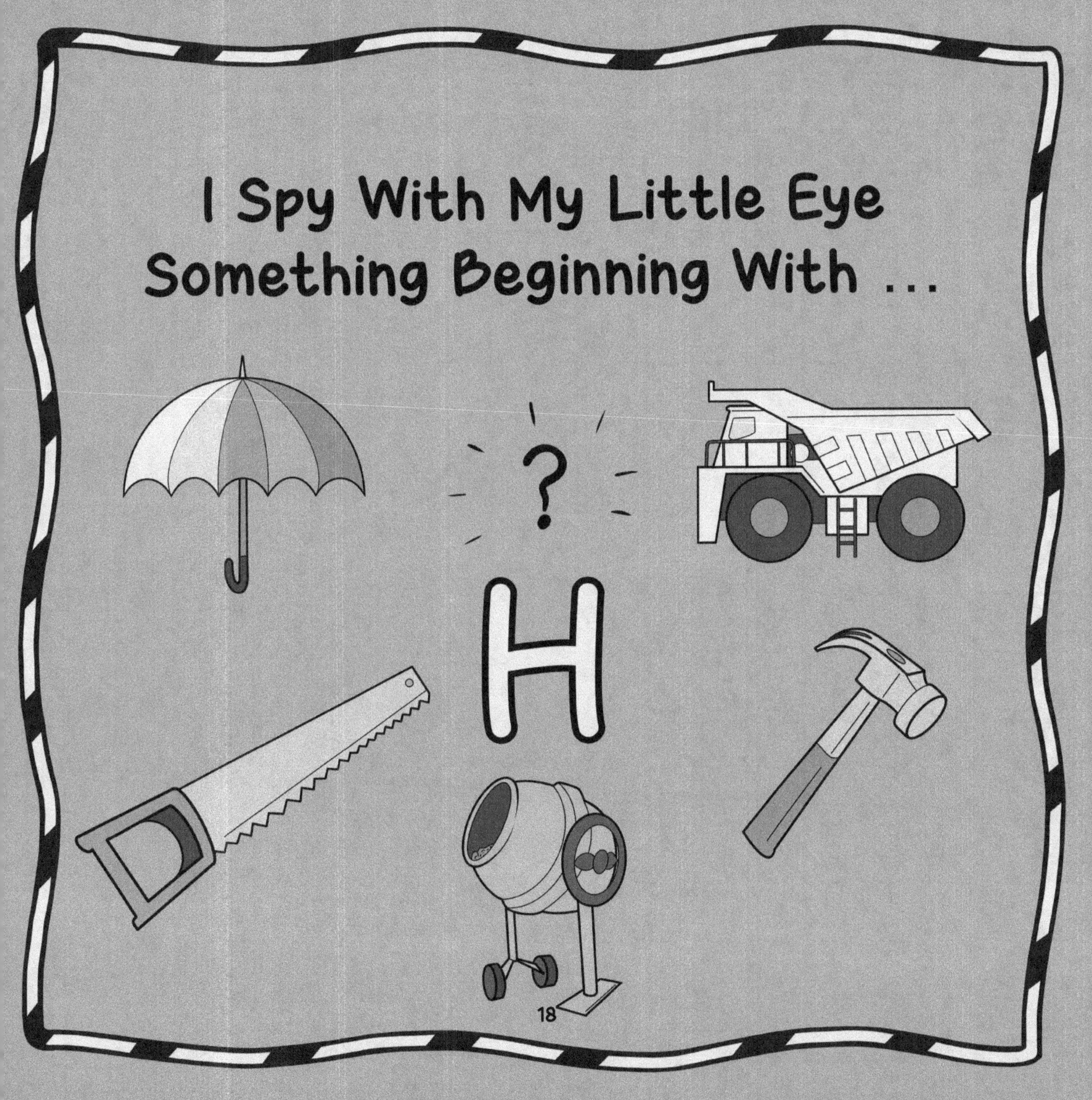
I Spy With My Little Eye
Something Beginning With ...
?
H
18

I spied a..

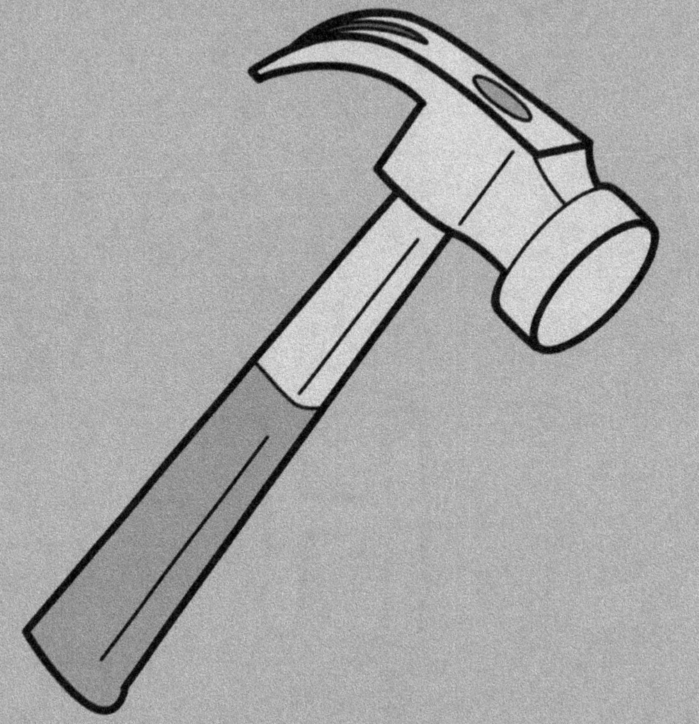

Hammer

I Spy With My Little Eye
Something Beginning With ...

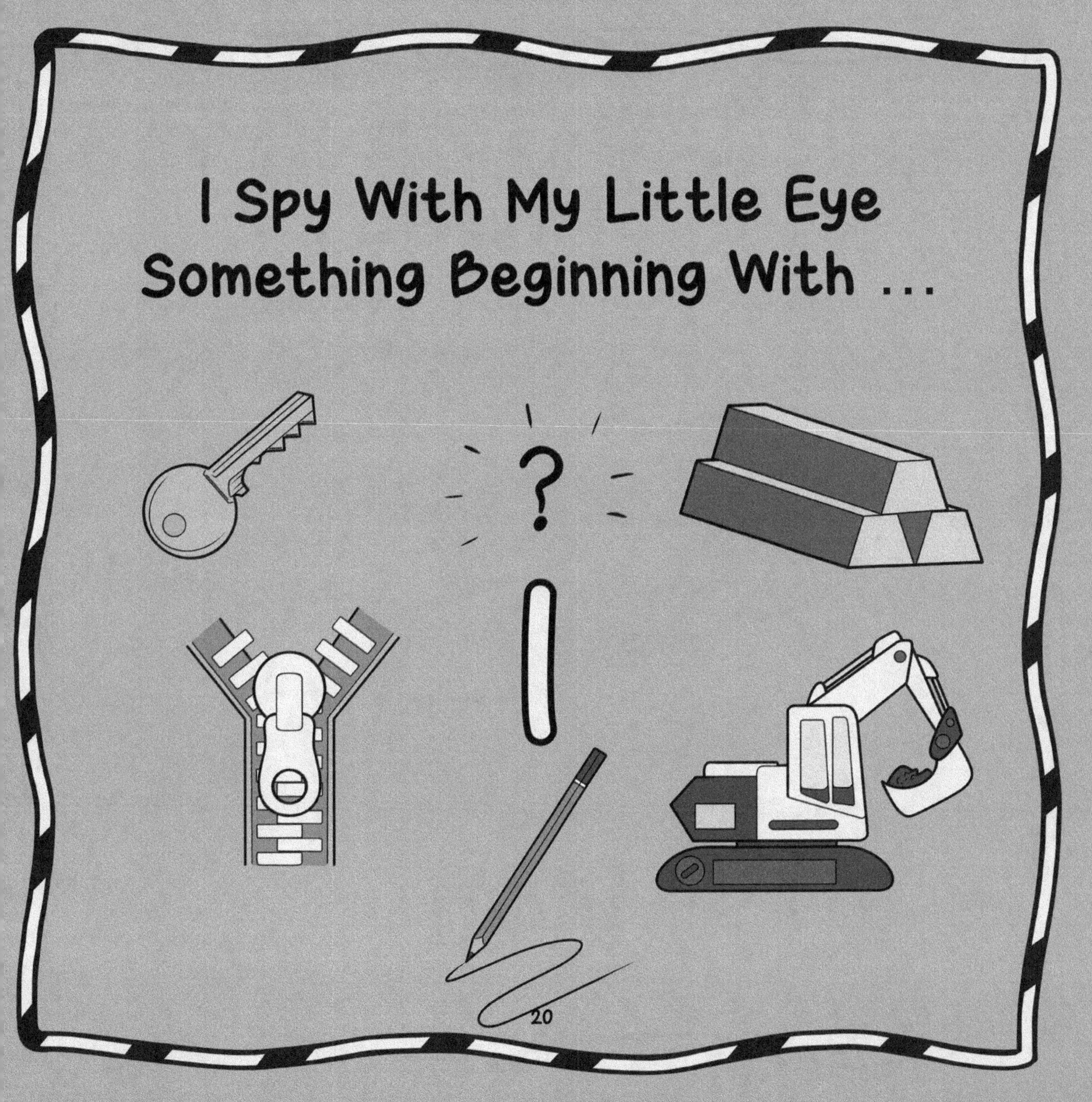

20

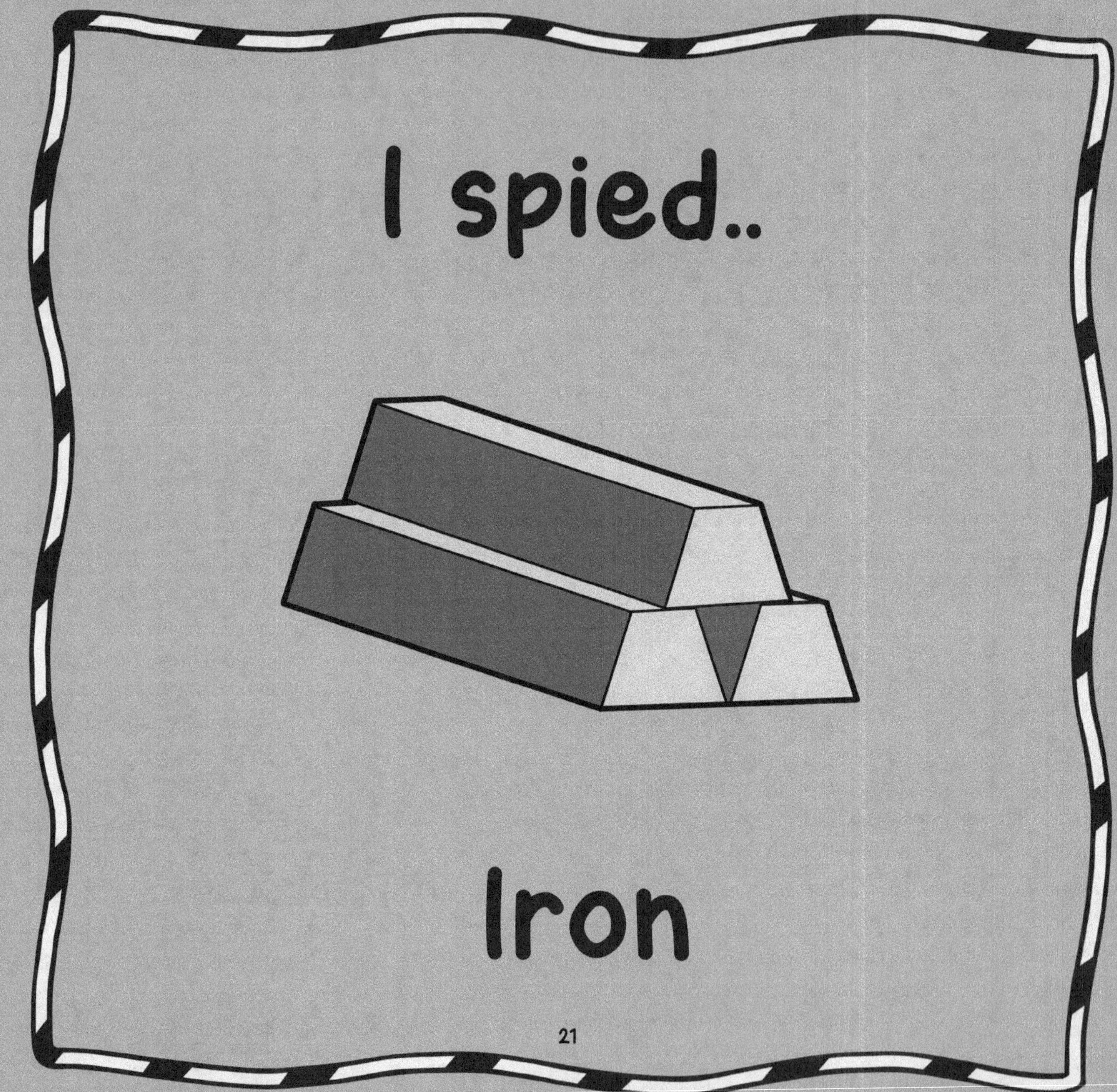
I spied..
Iron

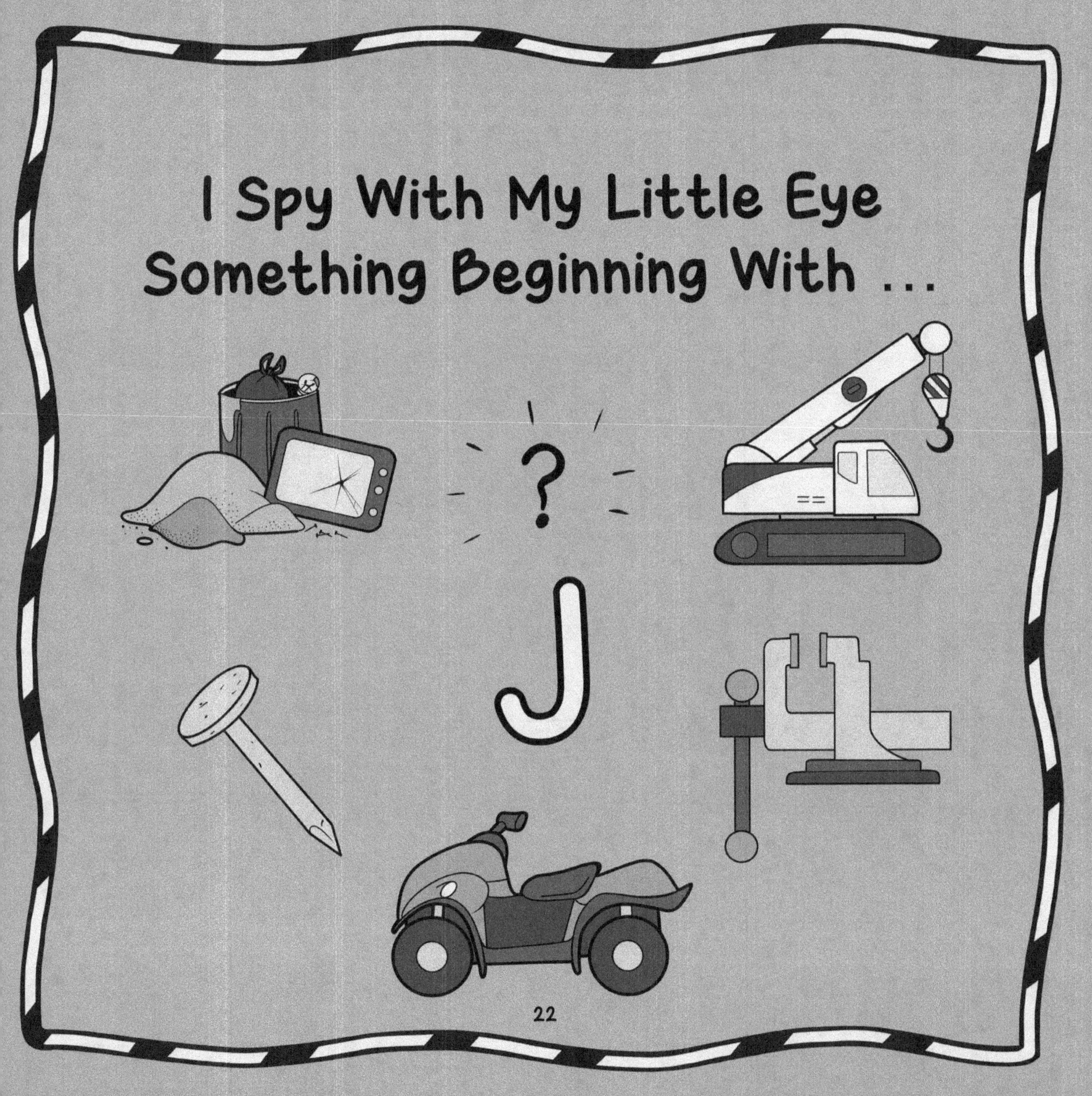

I Spy With My Little Eye
Something Beginning With ...
?
J

I spied..

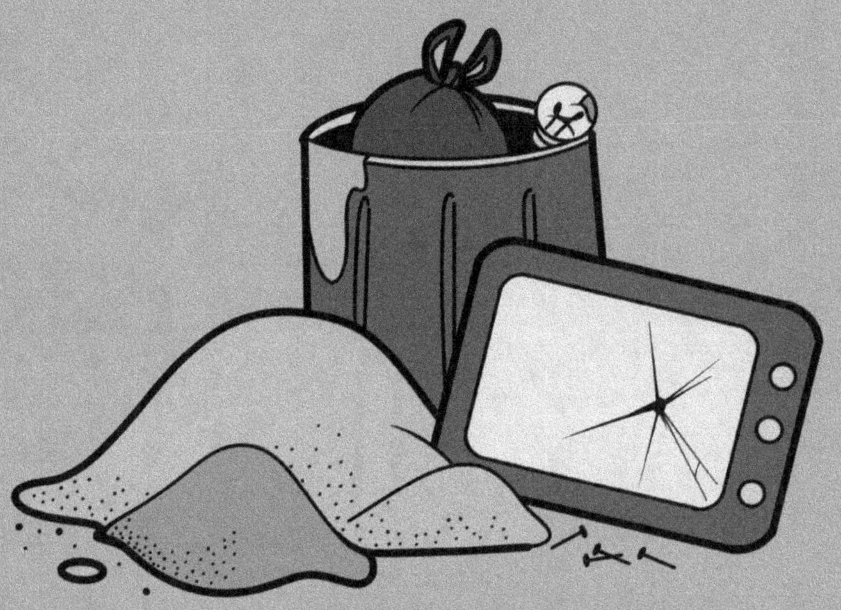

Junk

I Spy With My Little Eye Something Beginning With ...

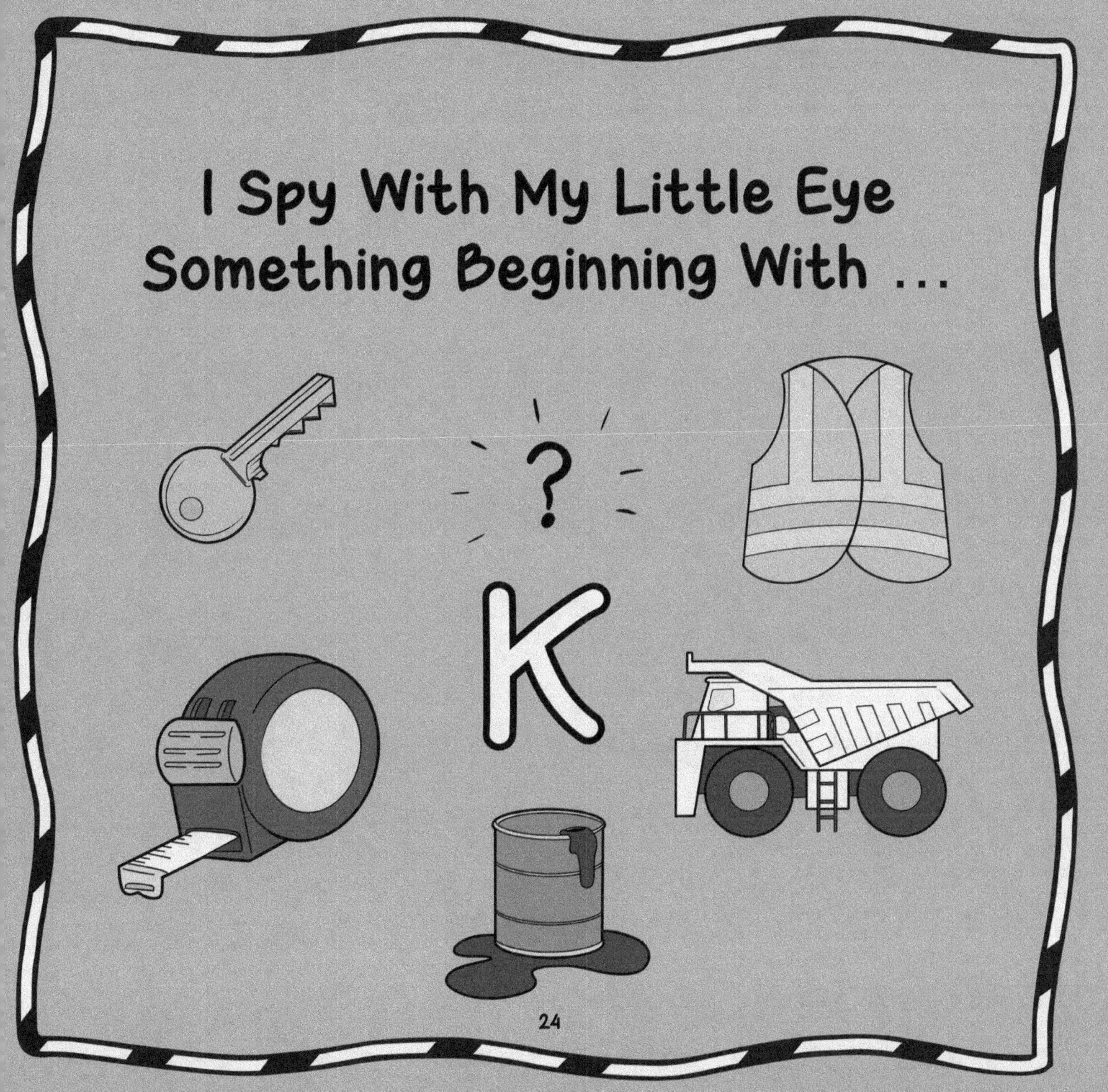

I spied a..

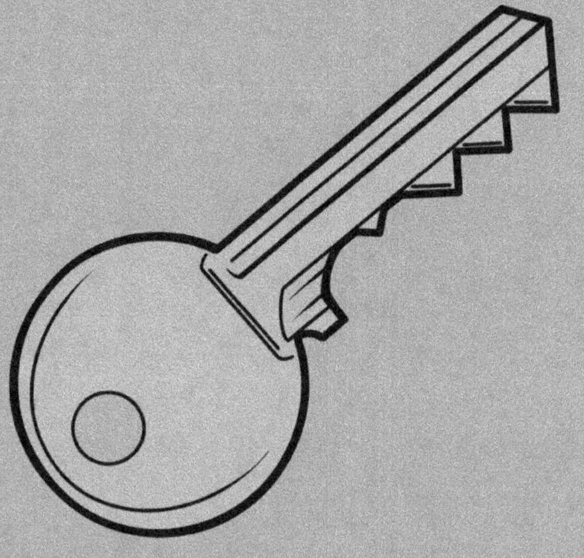

Key

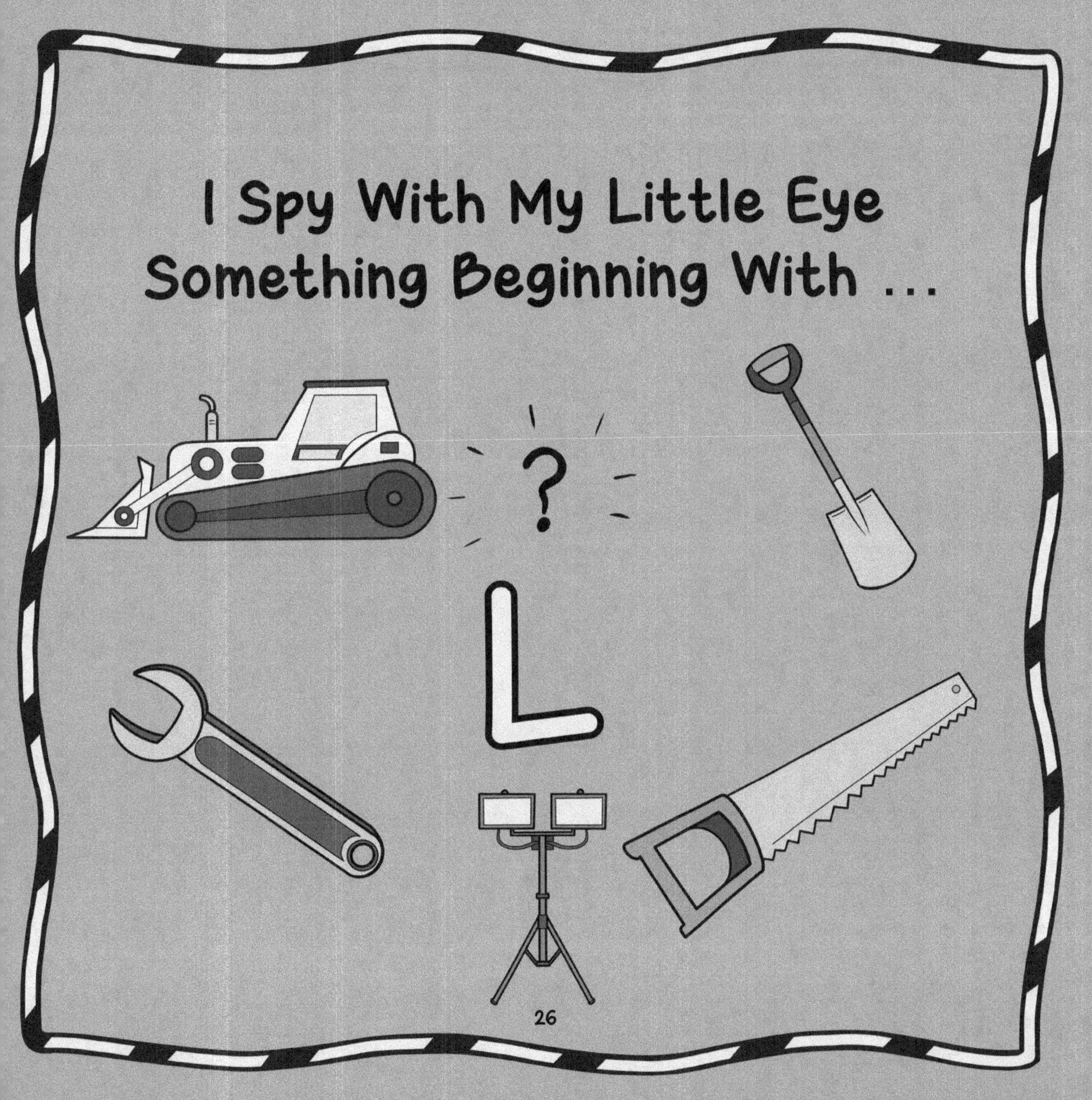

I Spy With My Little Eye
Something Beginning With ...
?
L
26

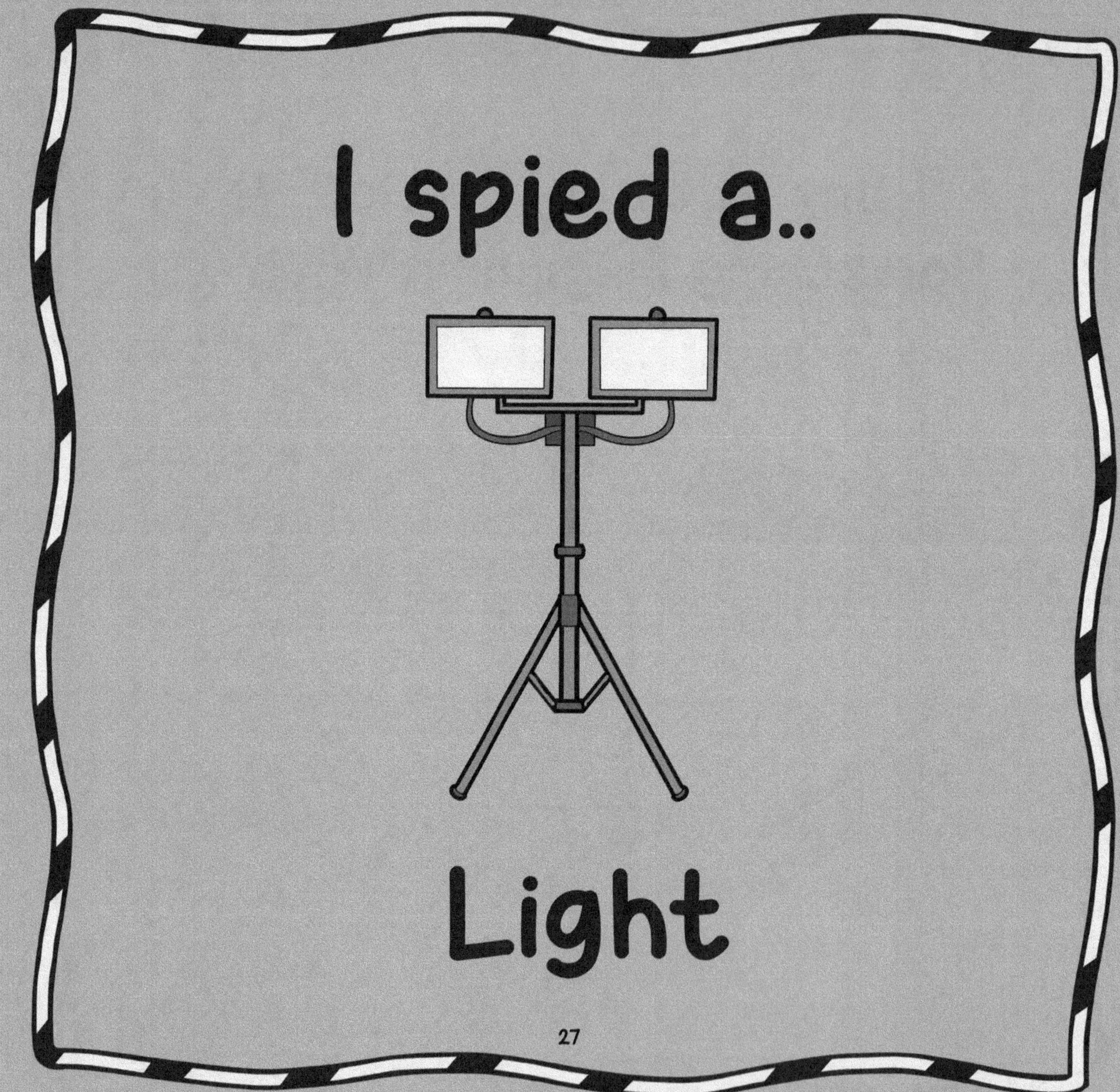
I spied a..
Light

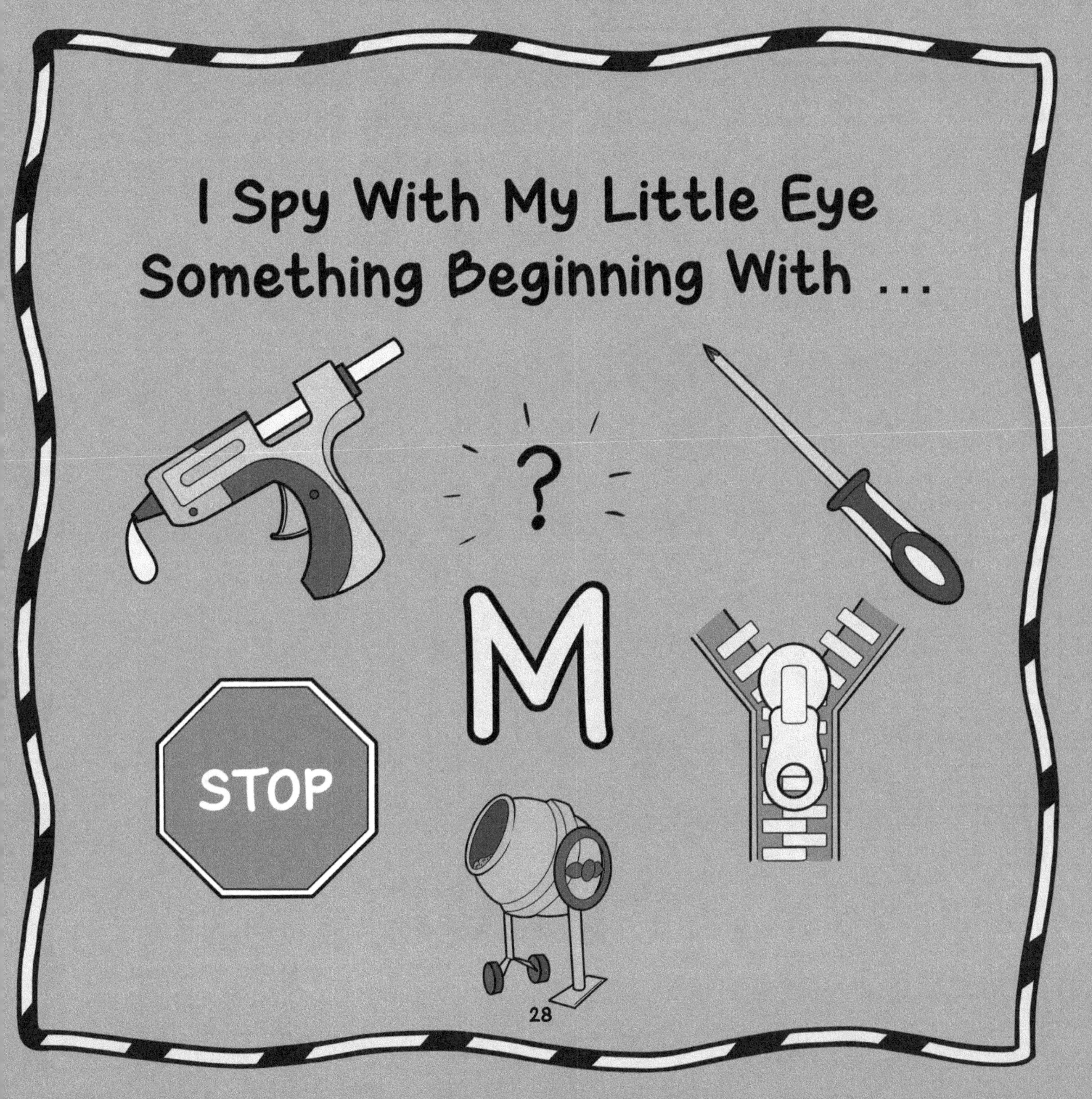

I Spy With My Little Eye
Something Beginning With ...
?
M
STOP
28

I spied a..

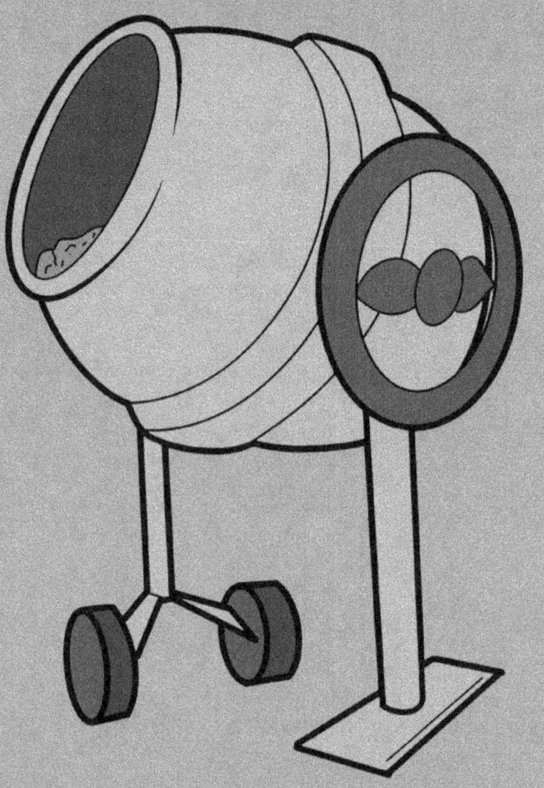

Mixer

I Spy With My Little Eye Something Beginning With ...

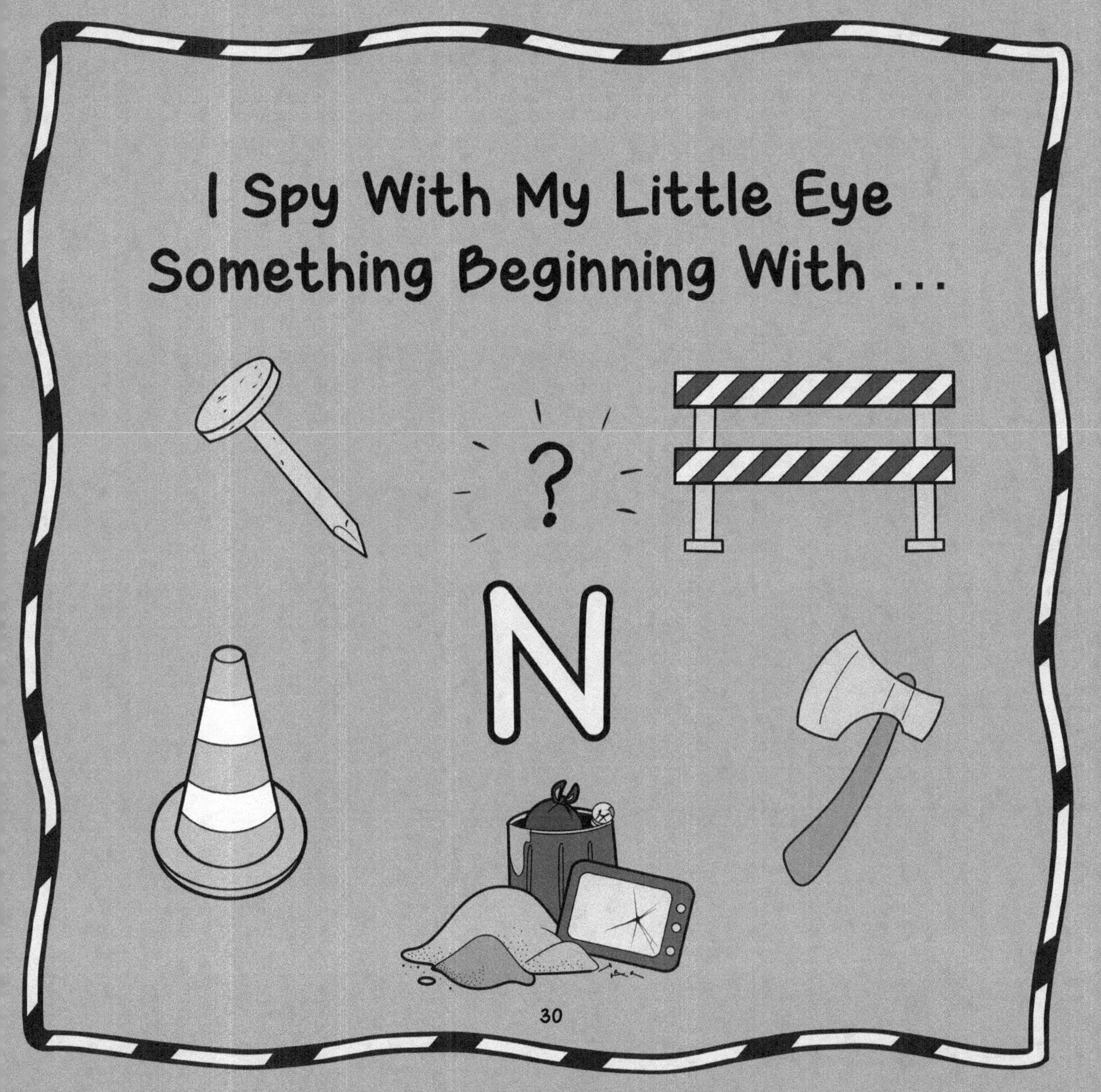

I spied a..

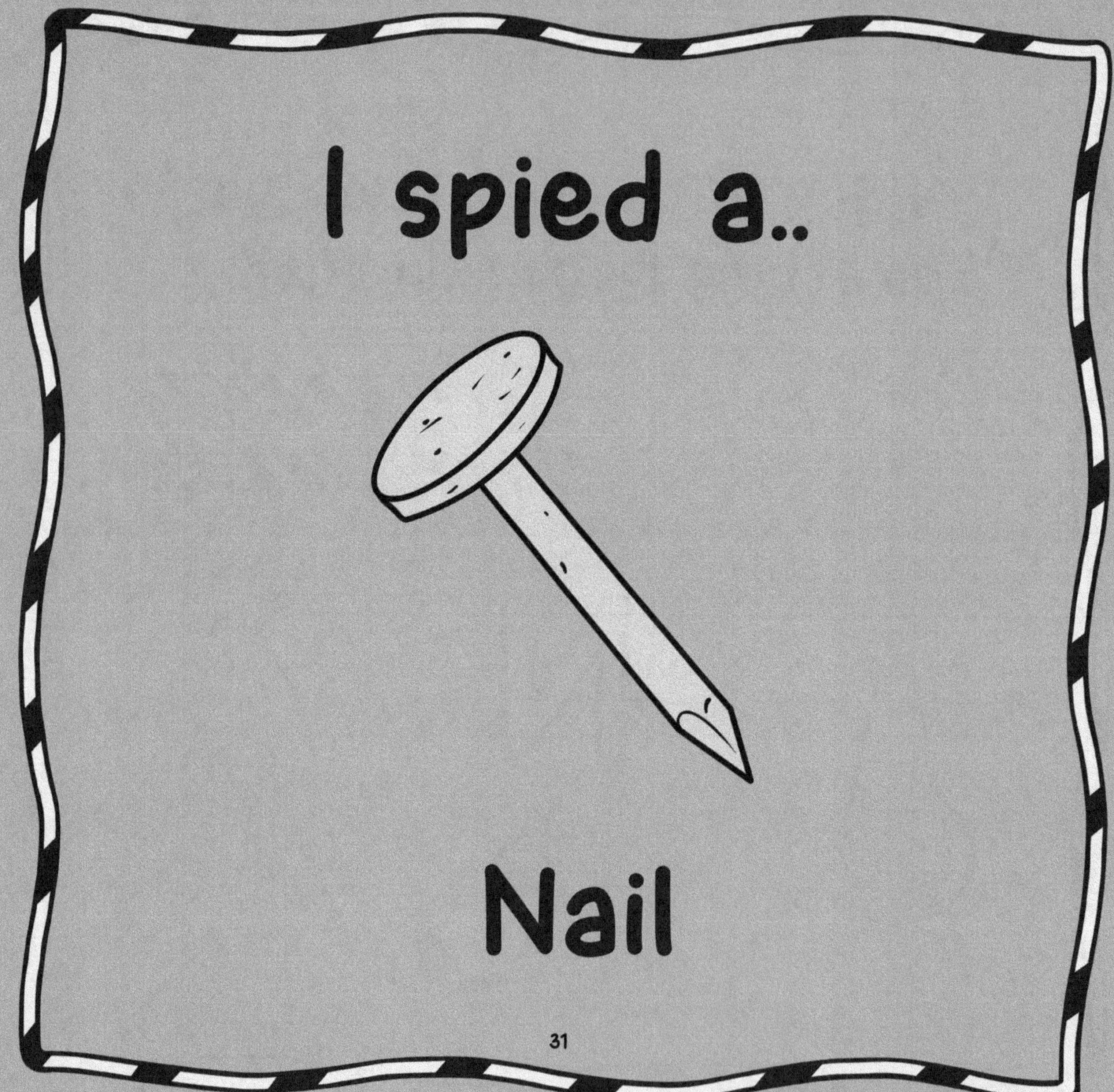

Nail

I Spy With My Little Eye Something Beginning With ...

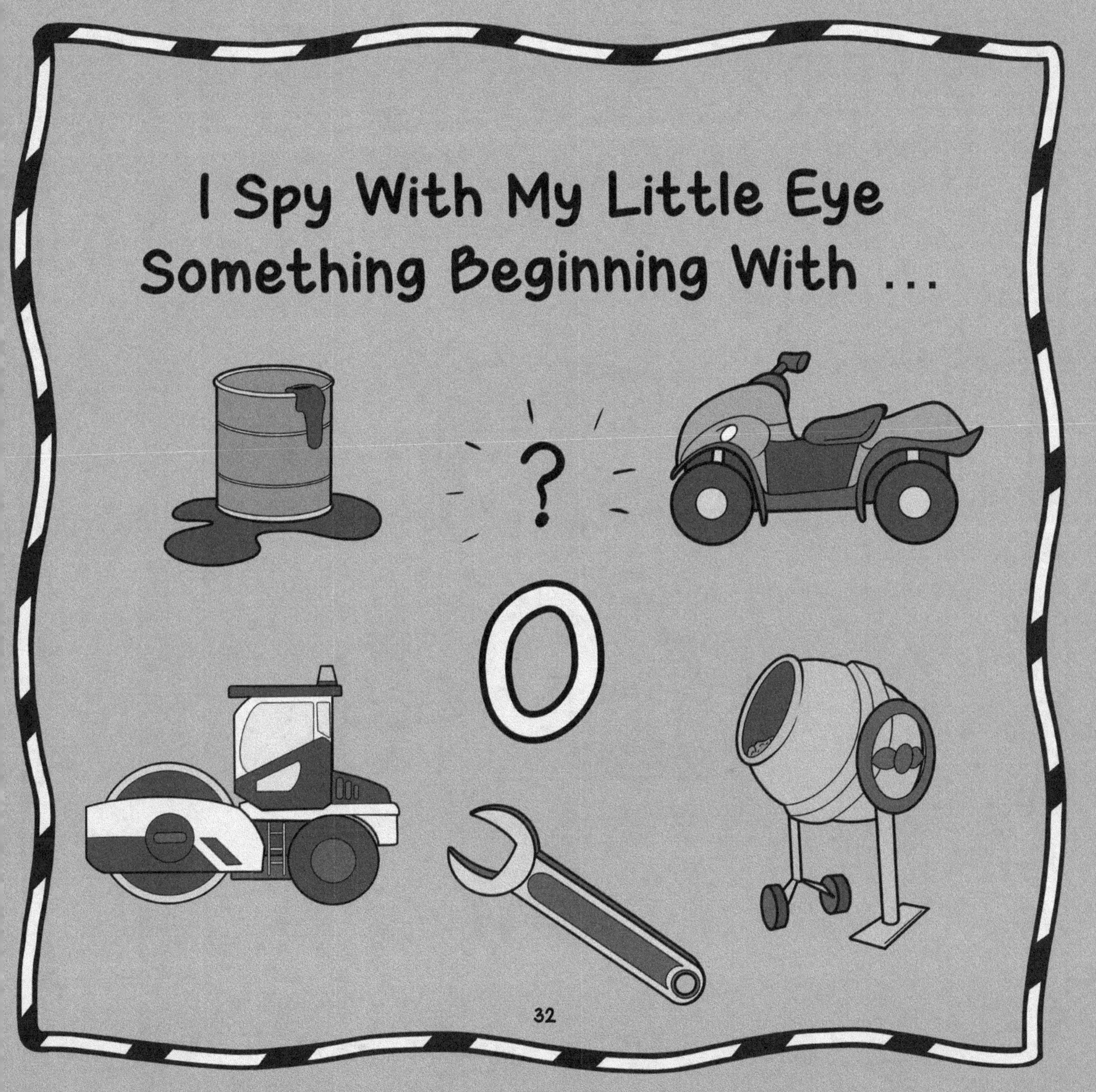

I spied..

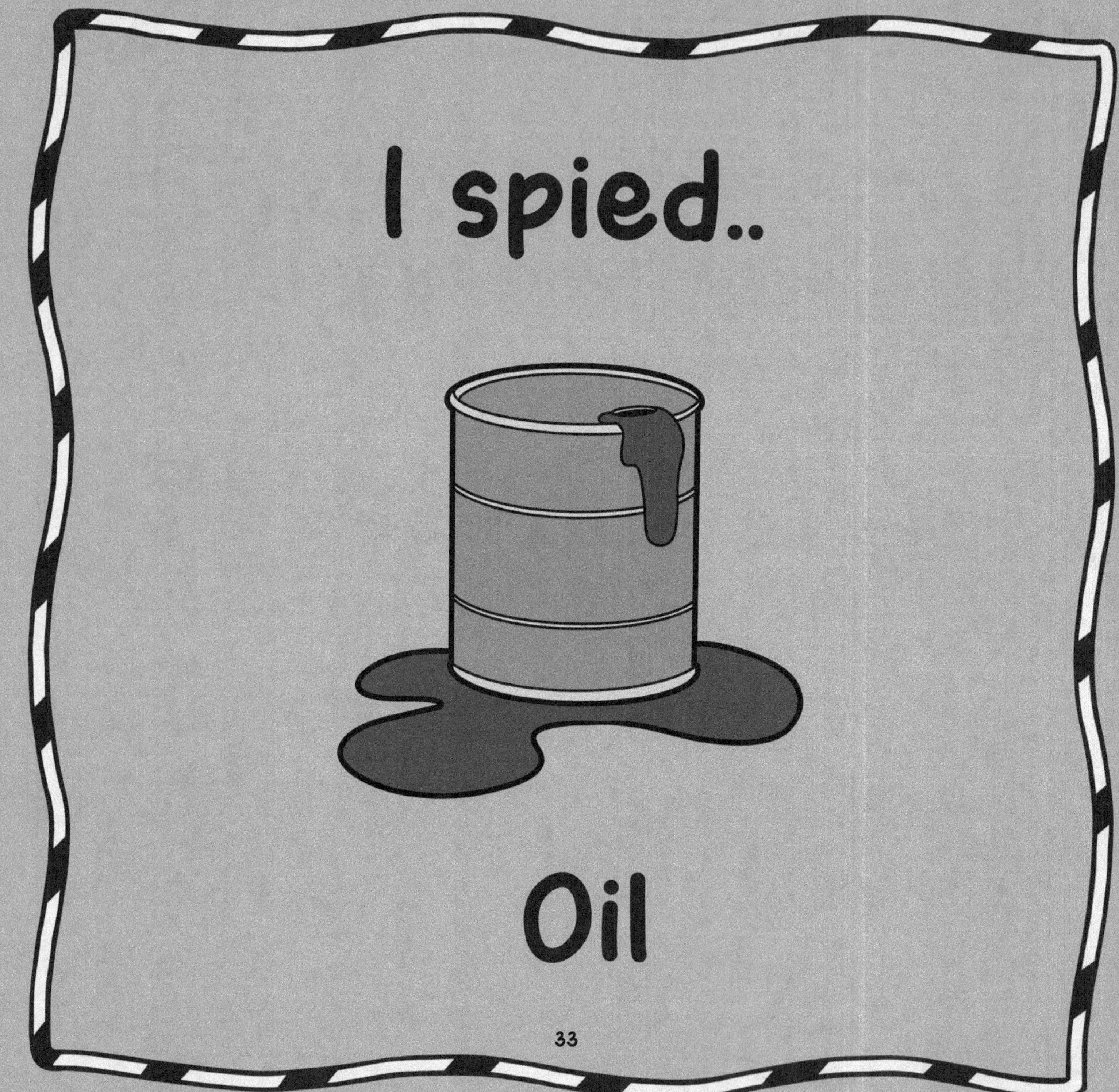

Oil

I Spy With My Little Eye Something Beginning With ...

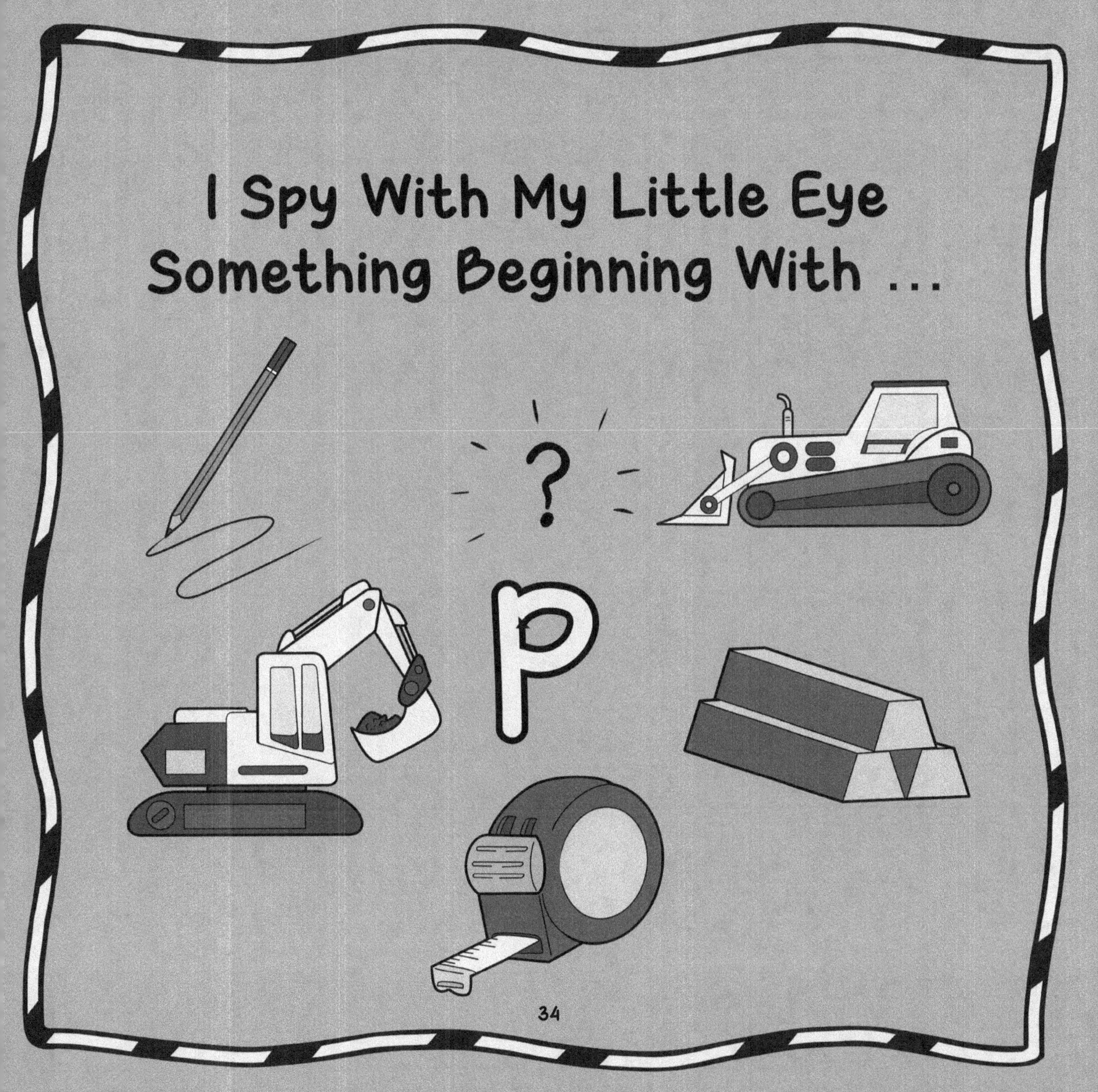

I spied a..

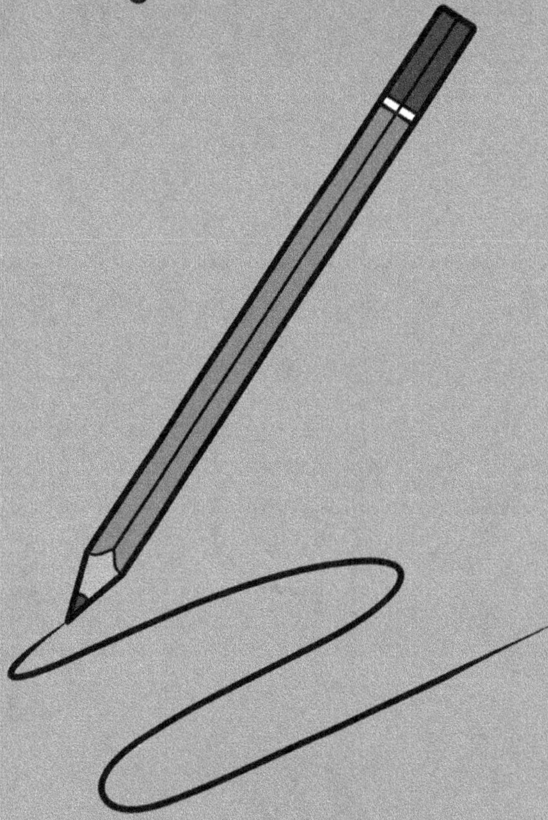

Pencil

I Spy With My Little Eye
Something Beginning With ...

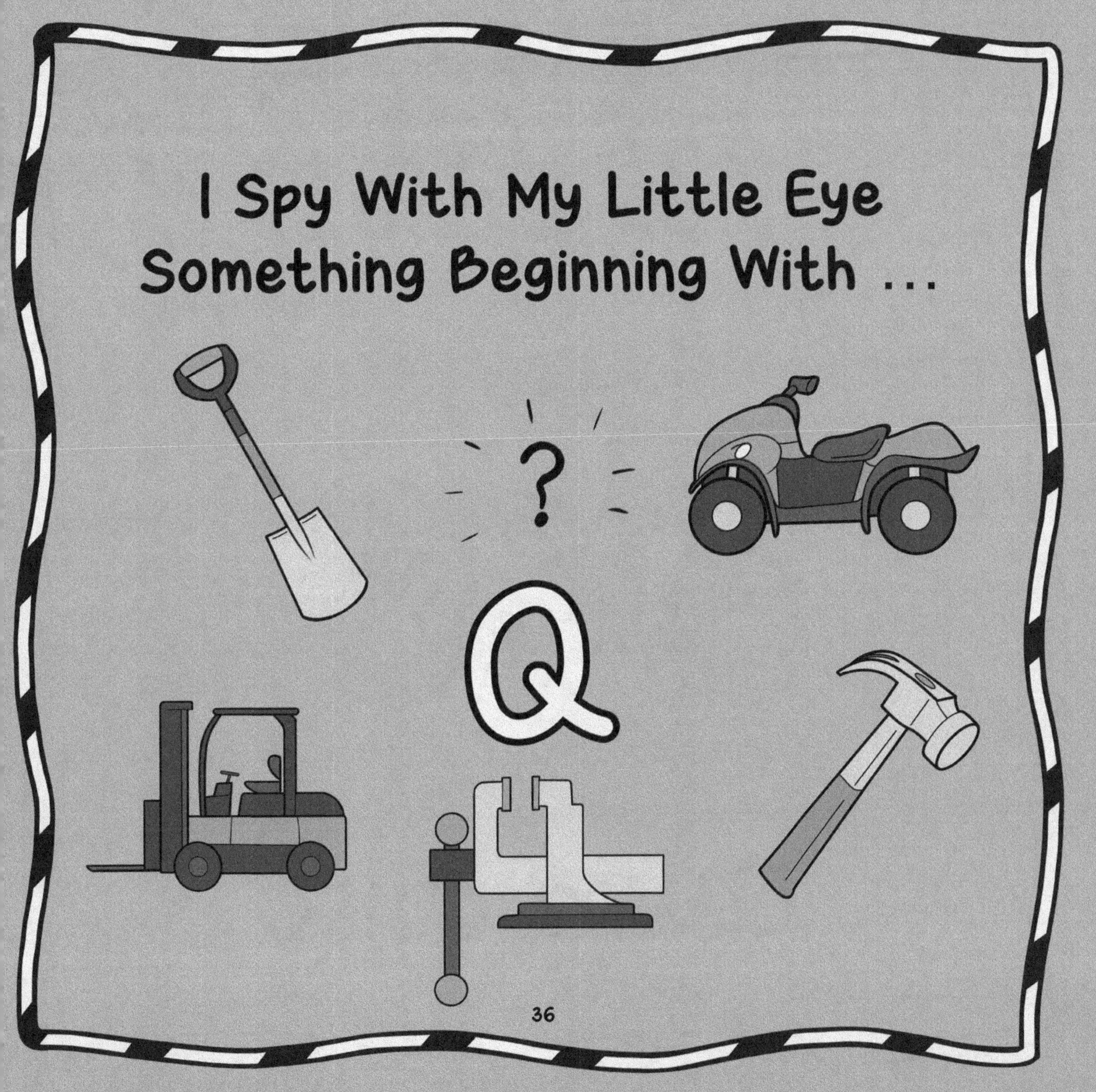

36

I spied a..

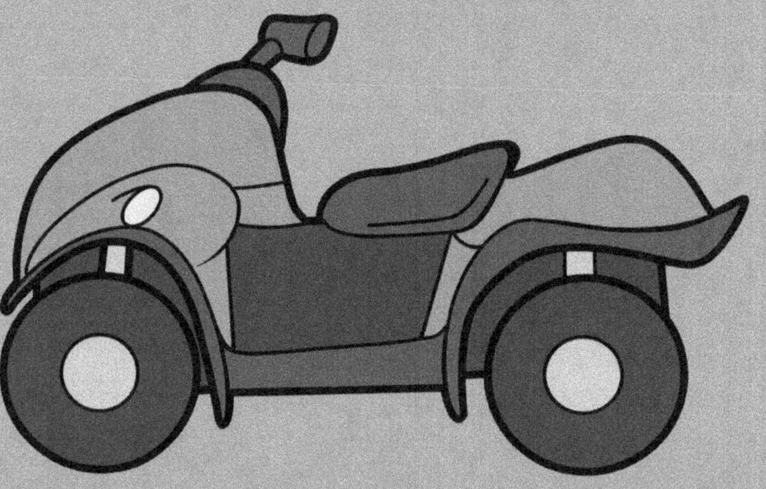

Quad Bike

I Spy With My Little Eye Something Beginning With ...

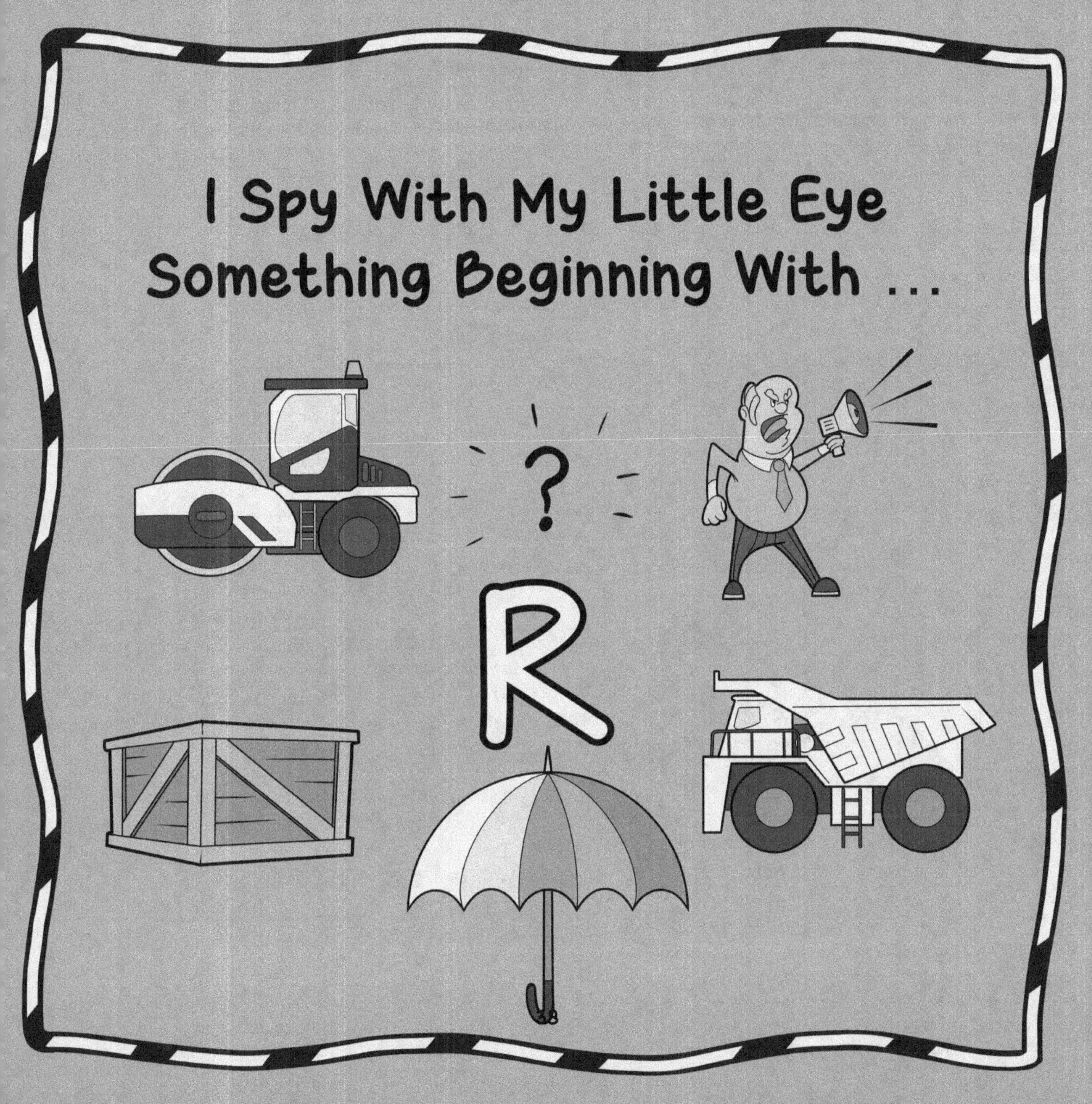

I spied a..

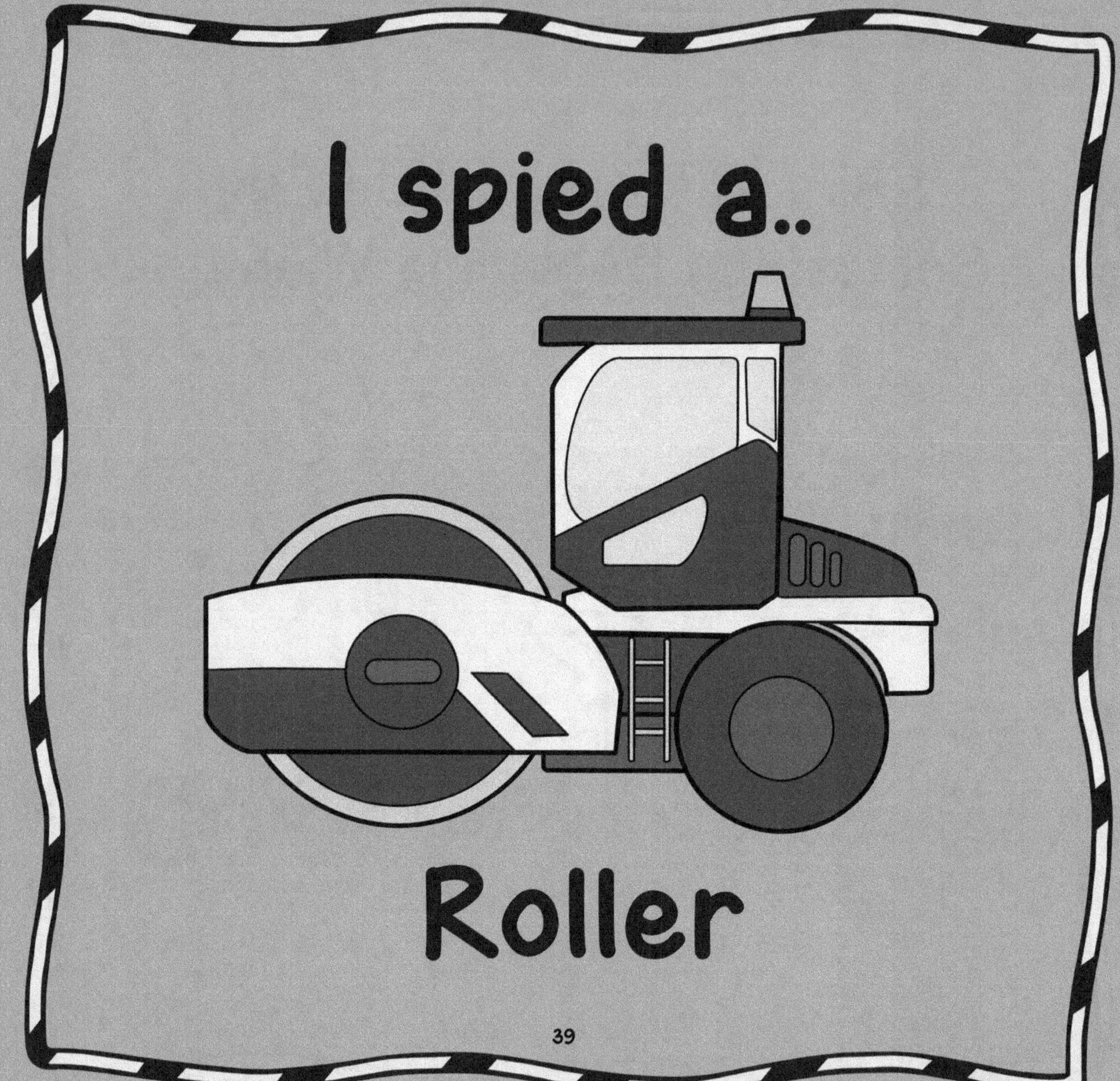

Roller

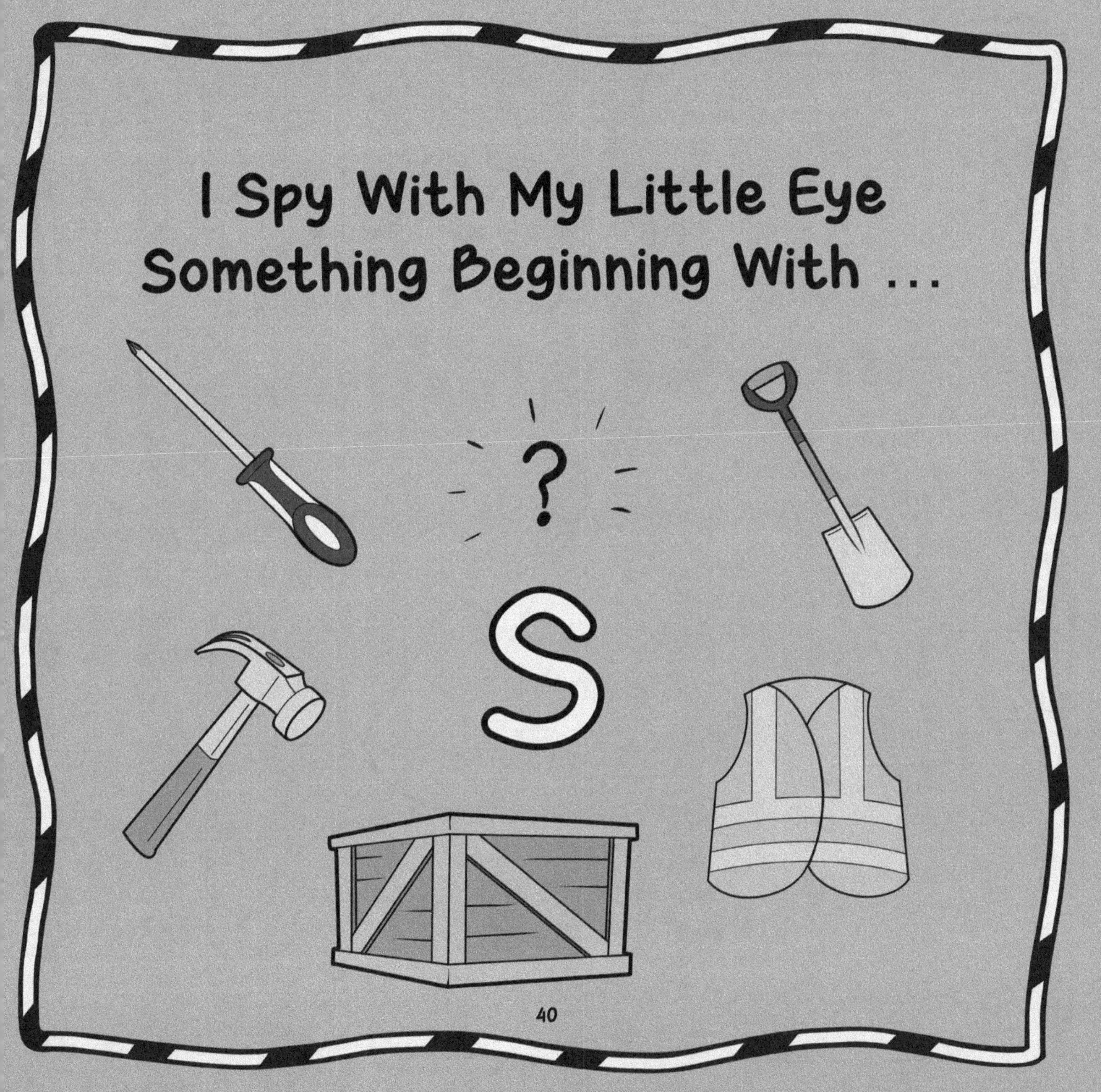

I Spy With My Little Eye
Something Beginning With ...
?
S
40

I spied a..

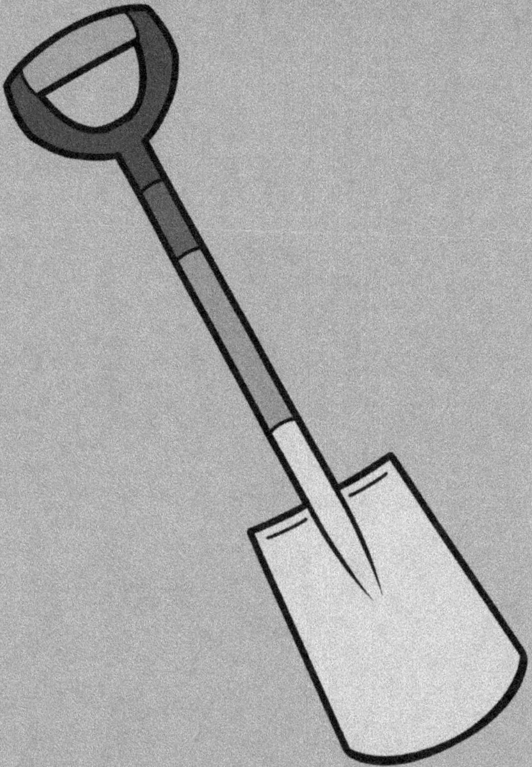

Shovel

I Spy With My Little Eye
Something Beginning With ...

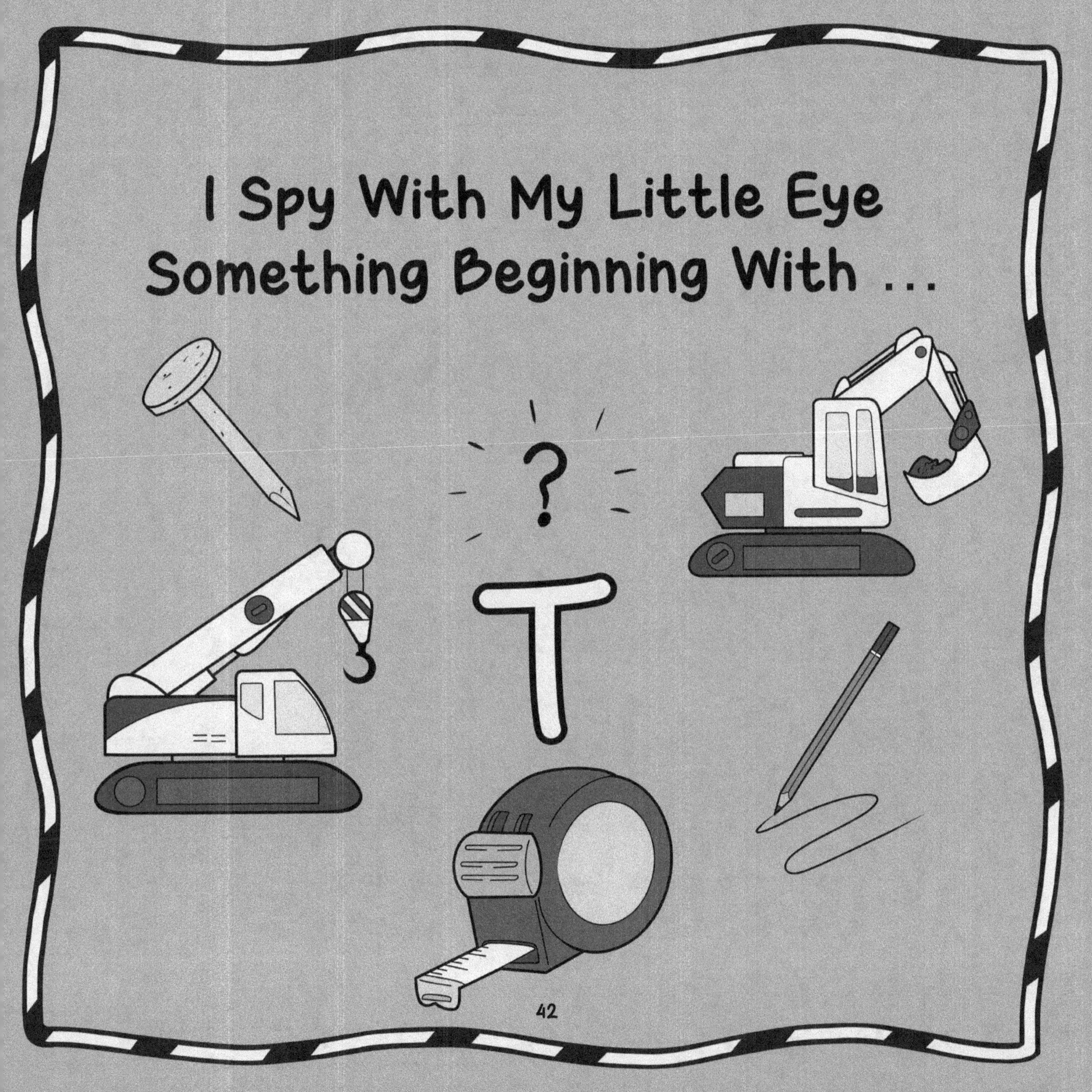

I spied a..

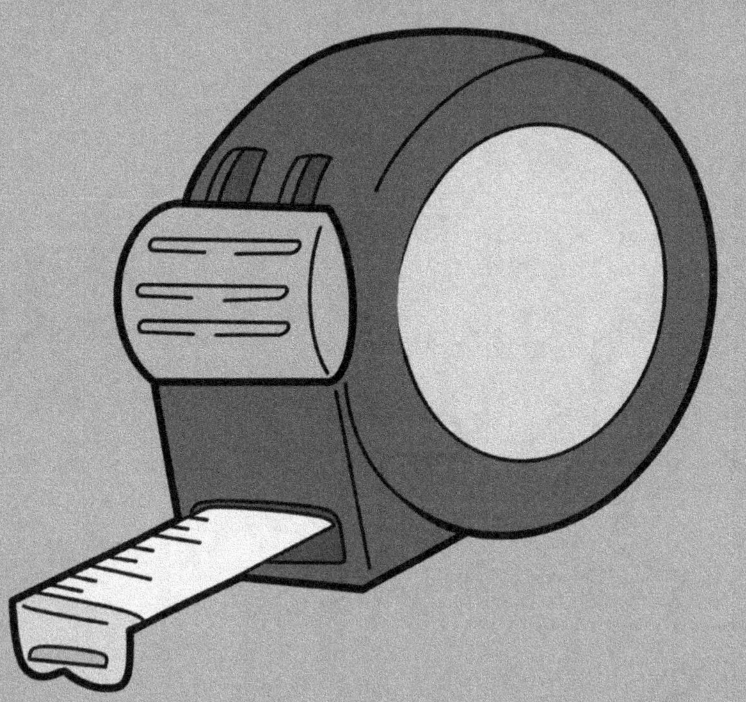

Tape measure

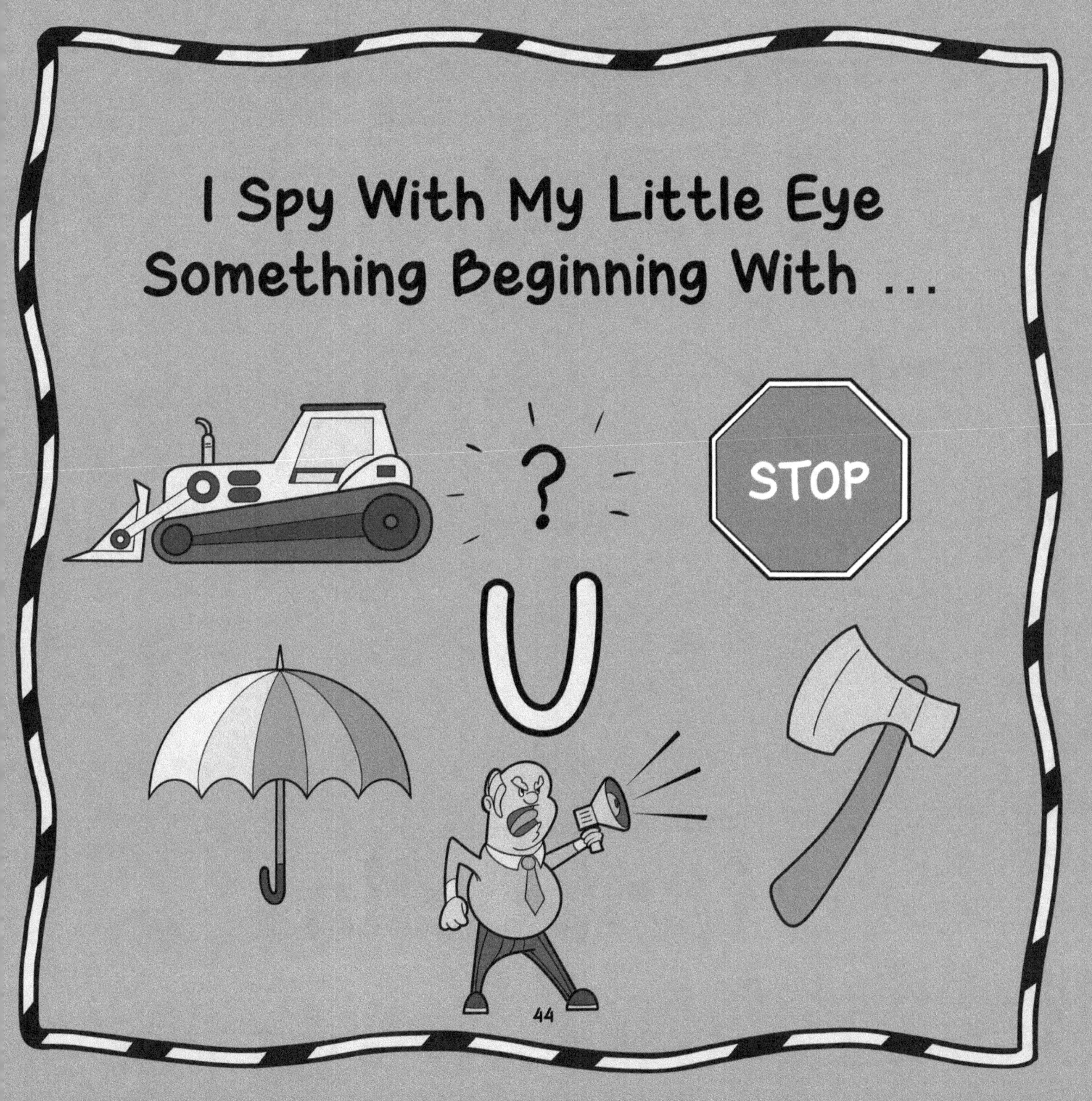

I Spy With My Little Eye
Something Beginning With ...
STOP
44

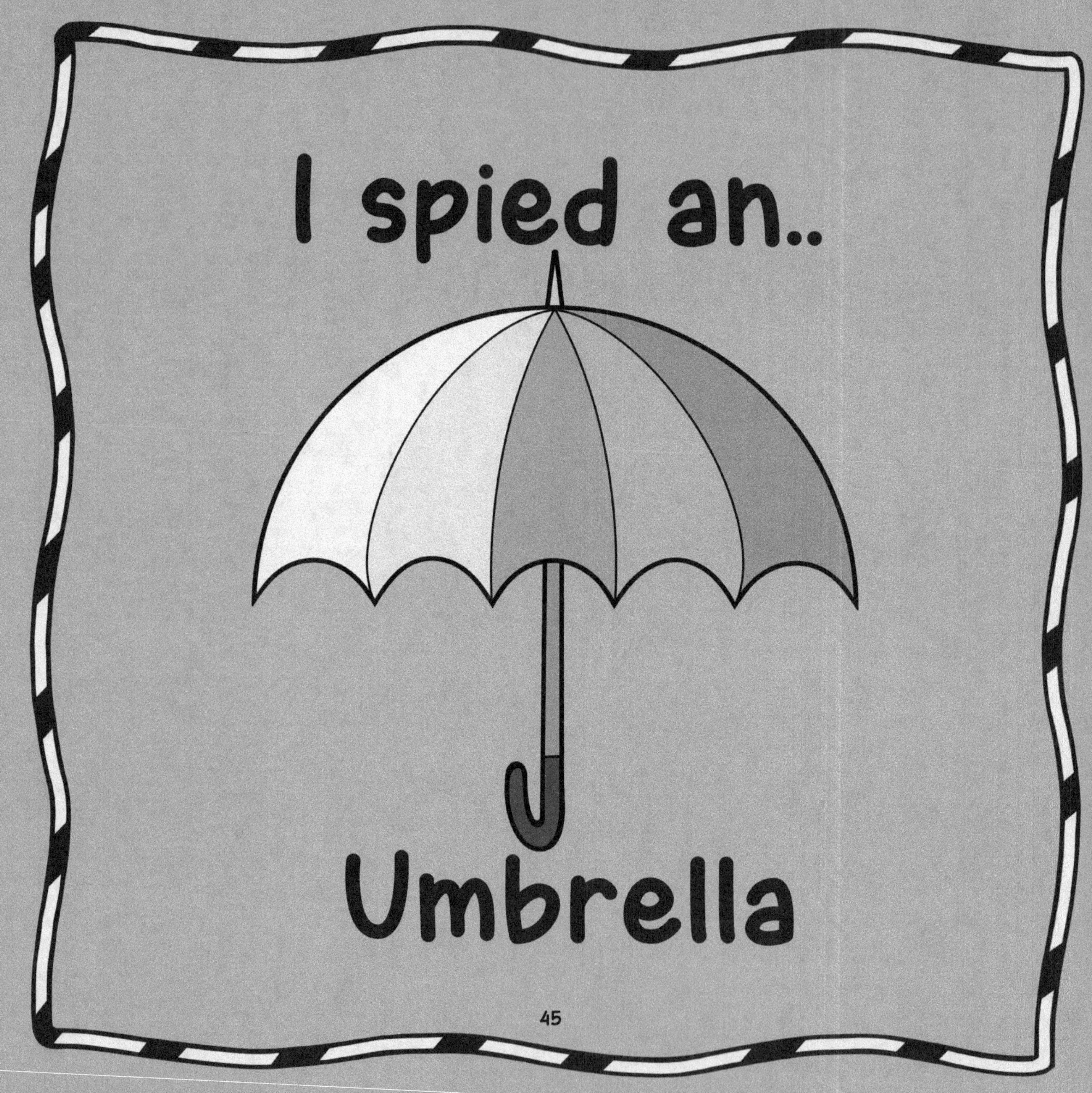

I spied an..
Umbrella
45

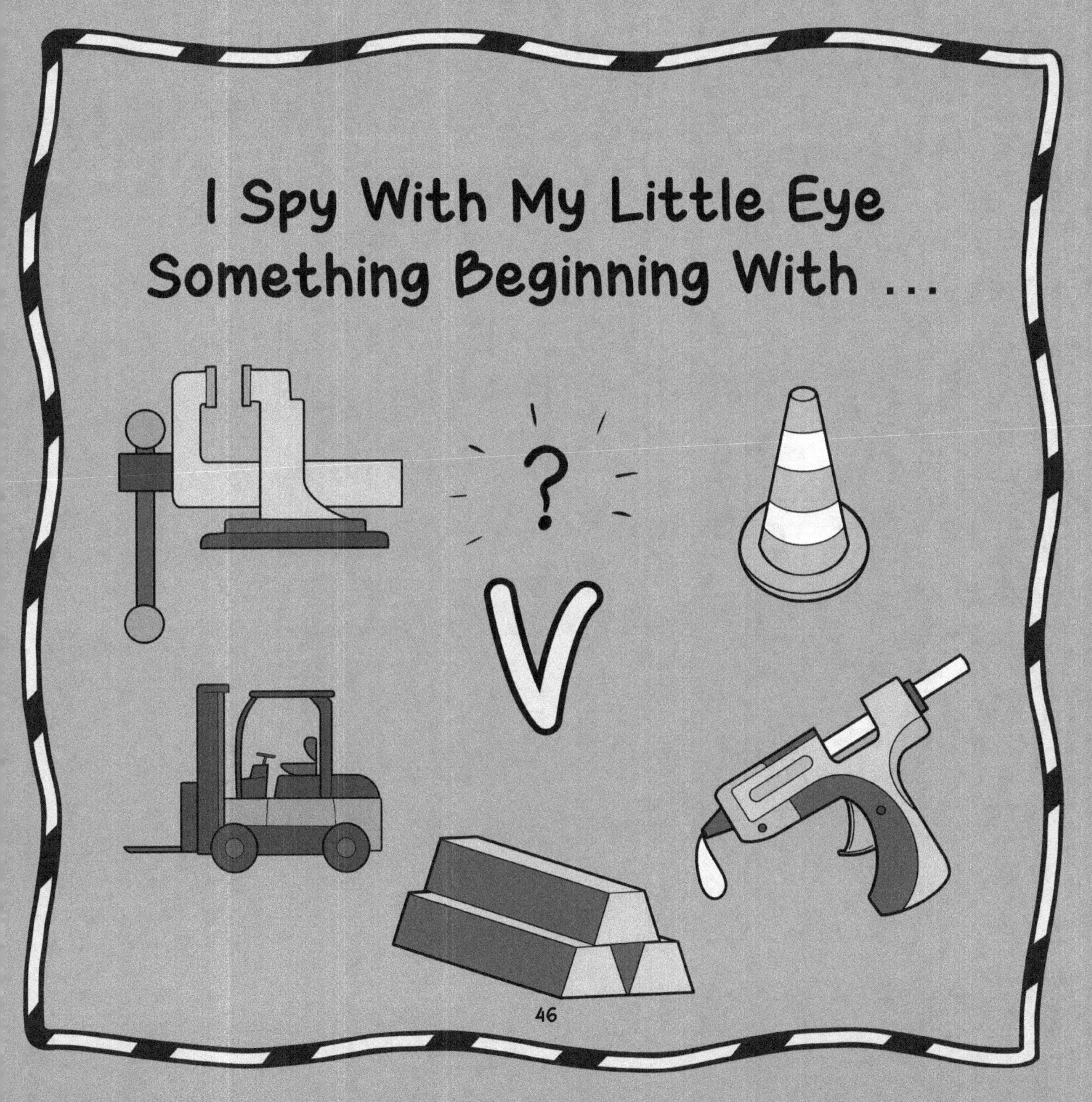

I Spy With My Little Eye
Something Beginning With ...
?
V
46

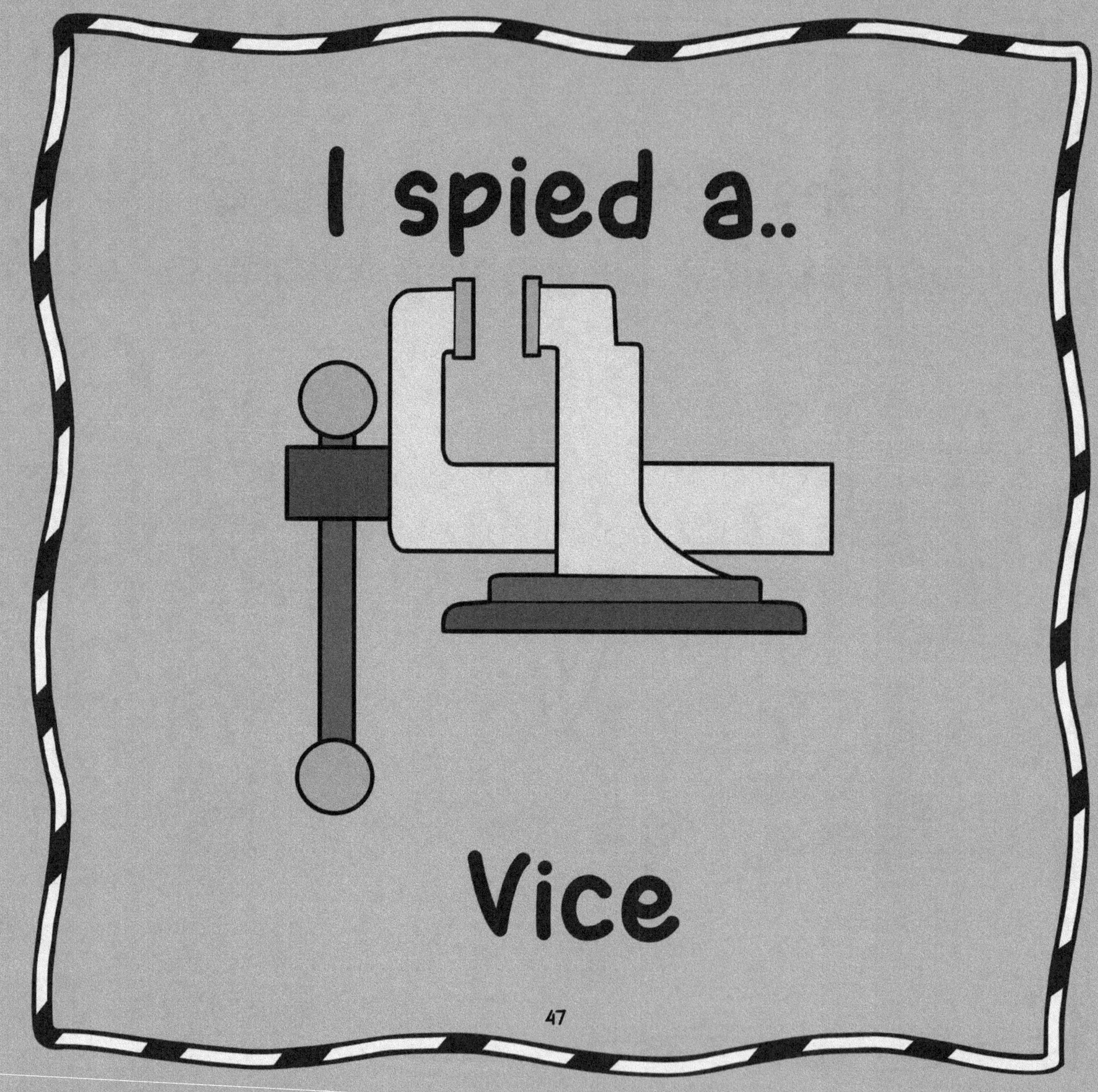

I spied a..
Vice

I Spy With My Little Eye Something Beginning With ...

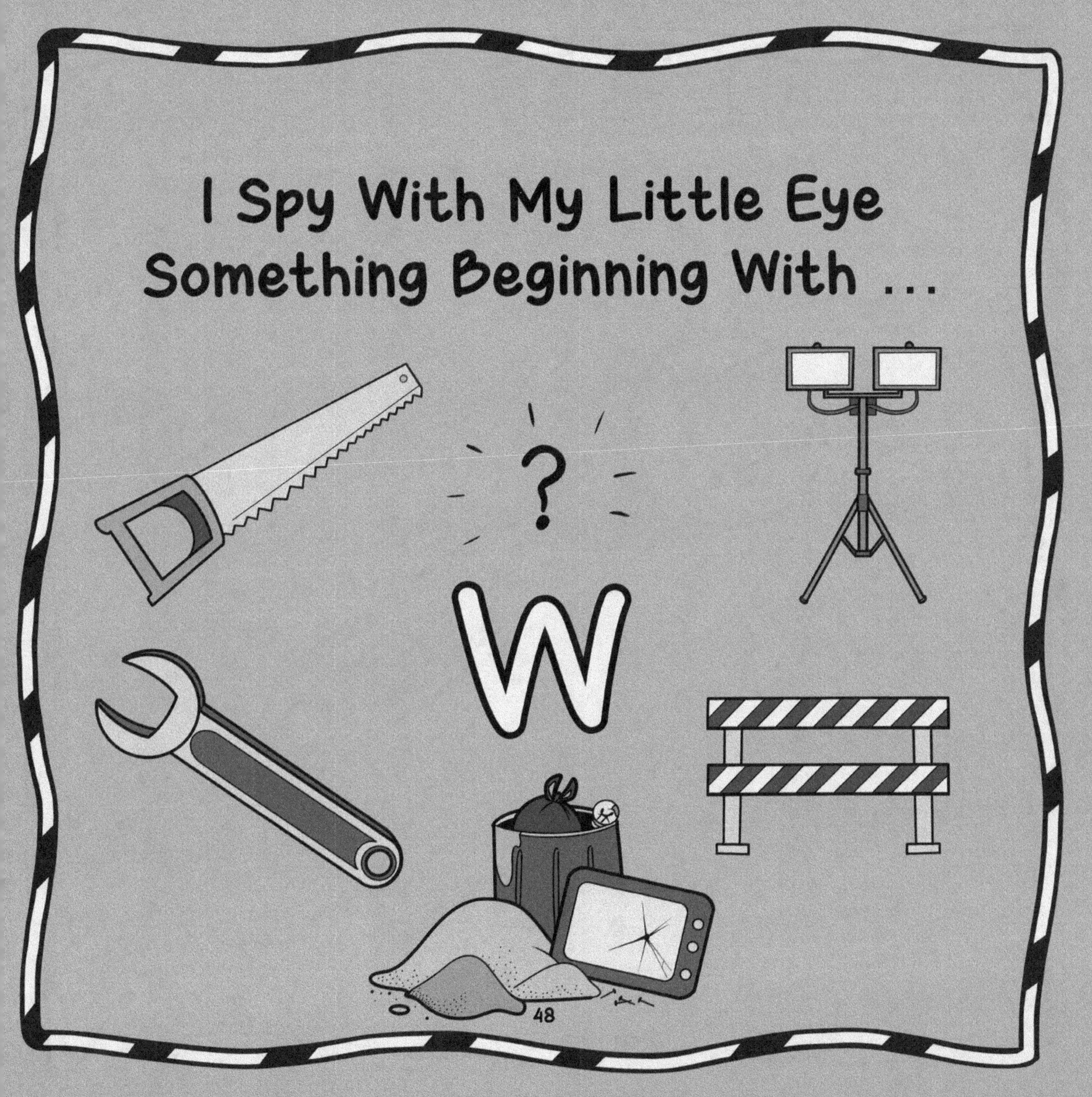

I spied a..

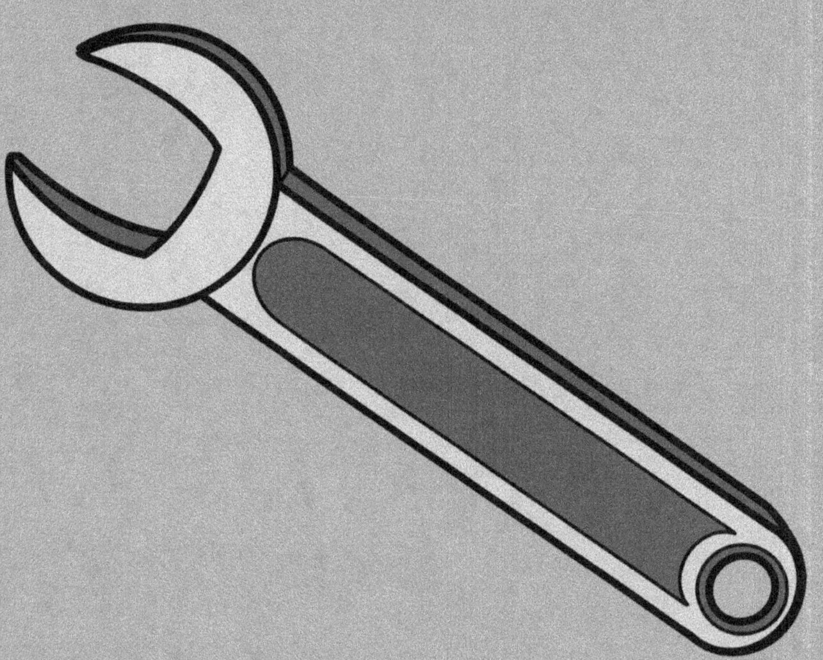

Wrench

I Spy With My Little Eye Something Ending With ...

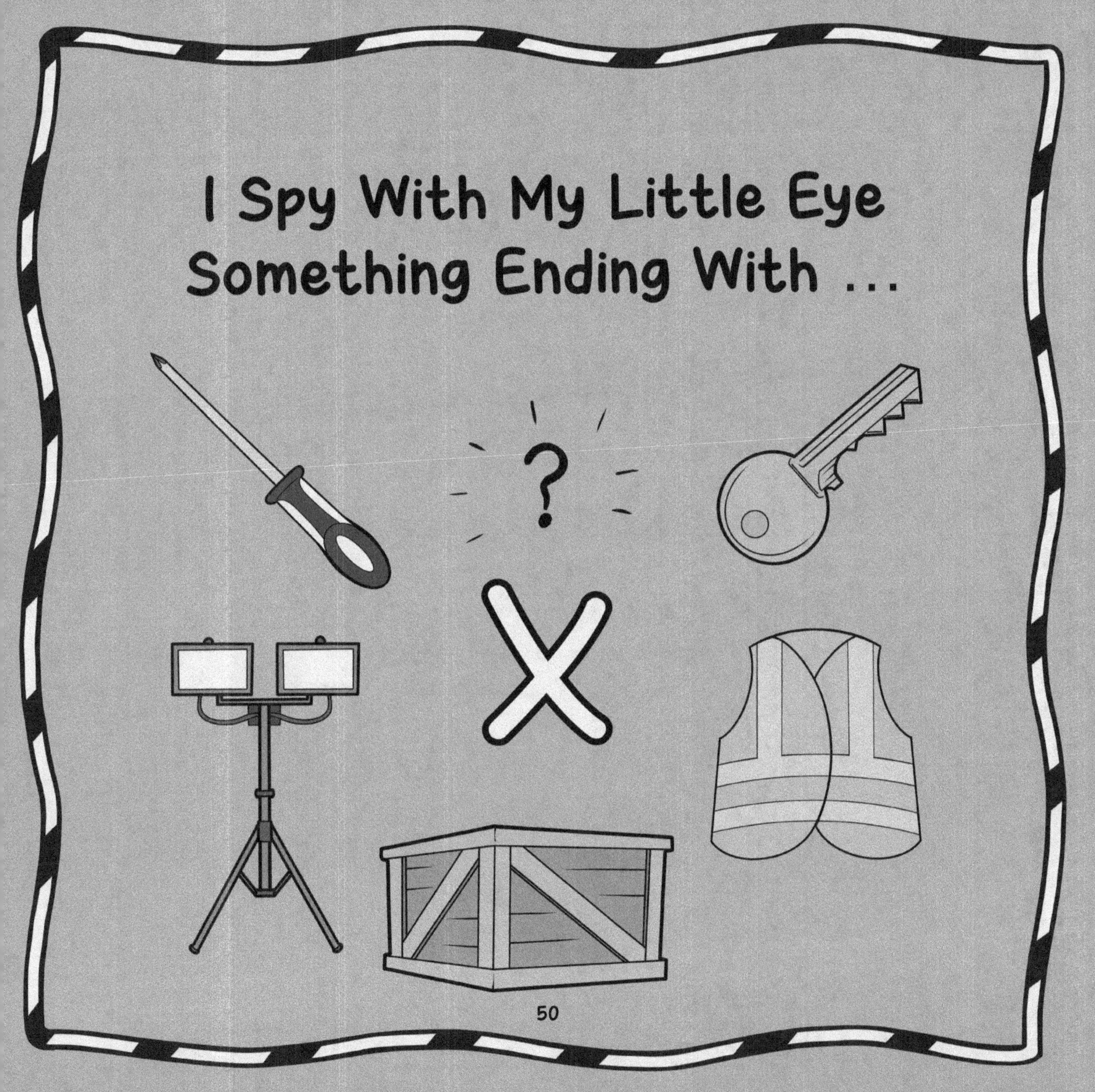

I spied a..

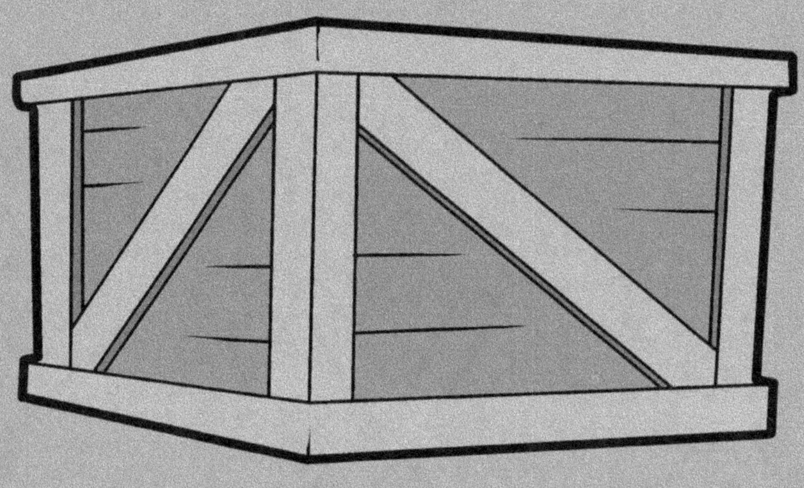

Box

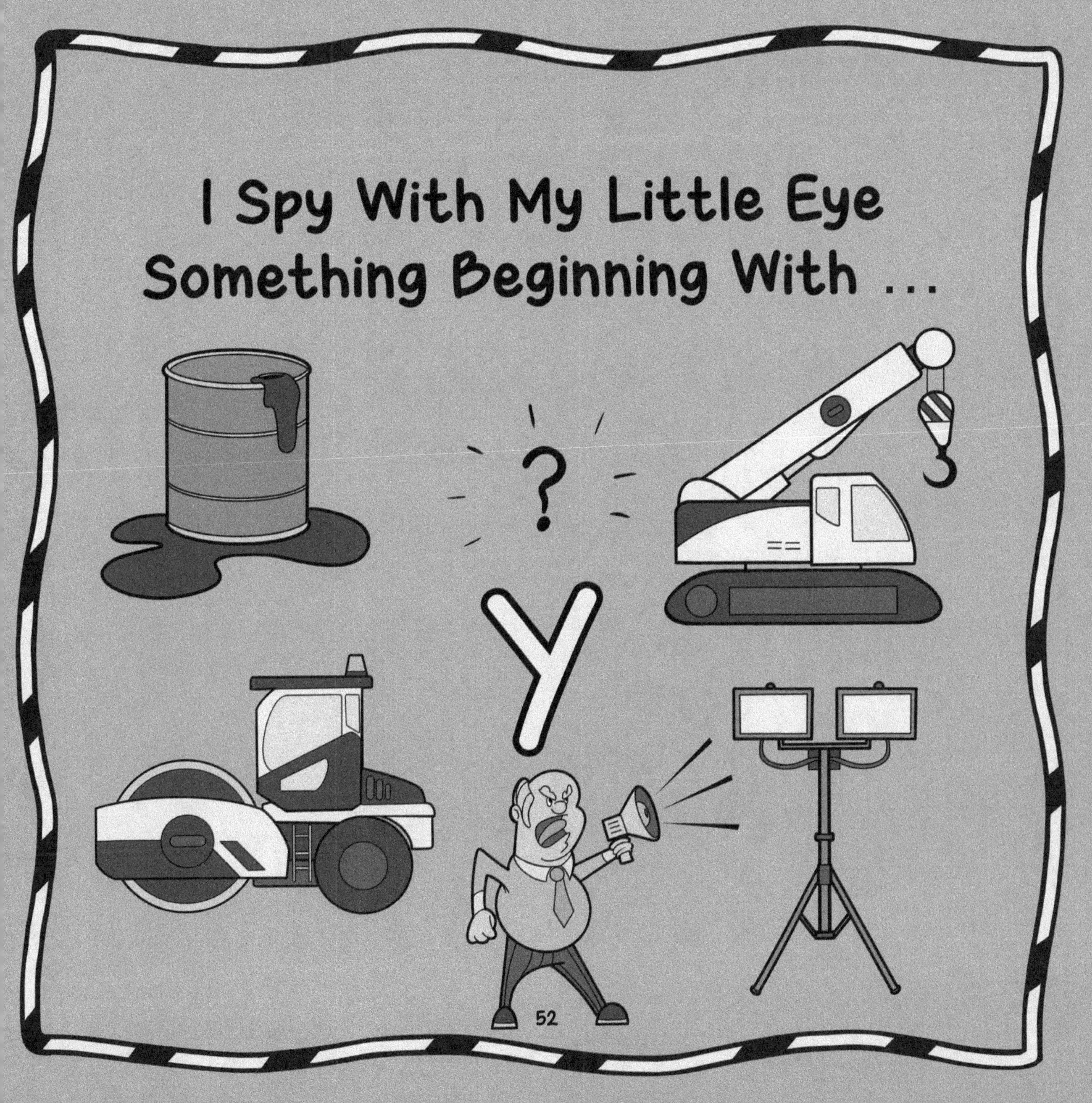

I Spy With My Little Eye
Something Beginning With ...
?
Y
52

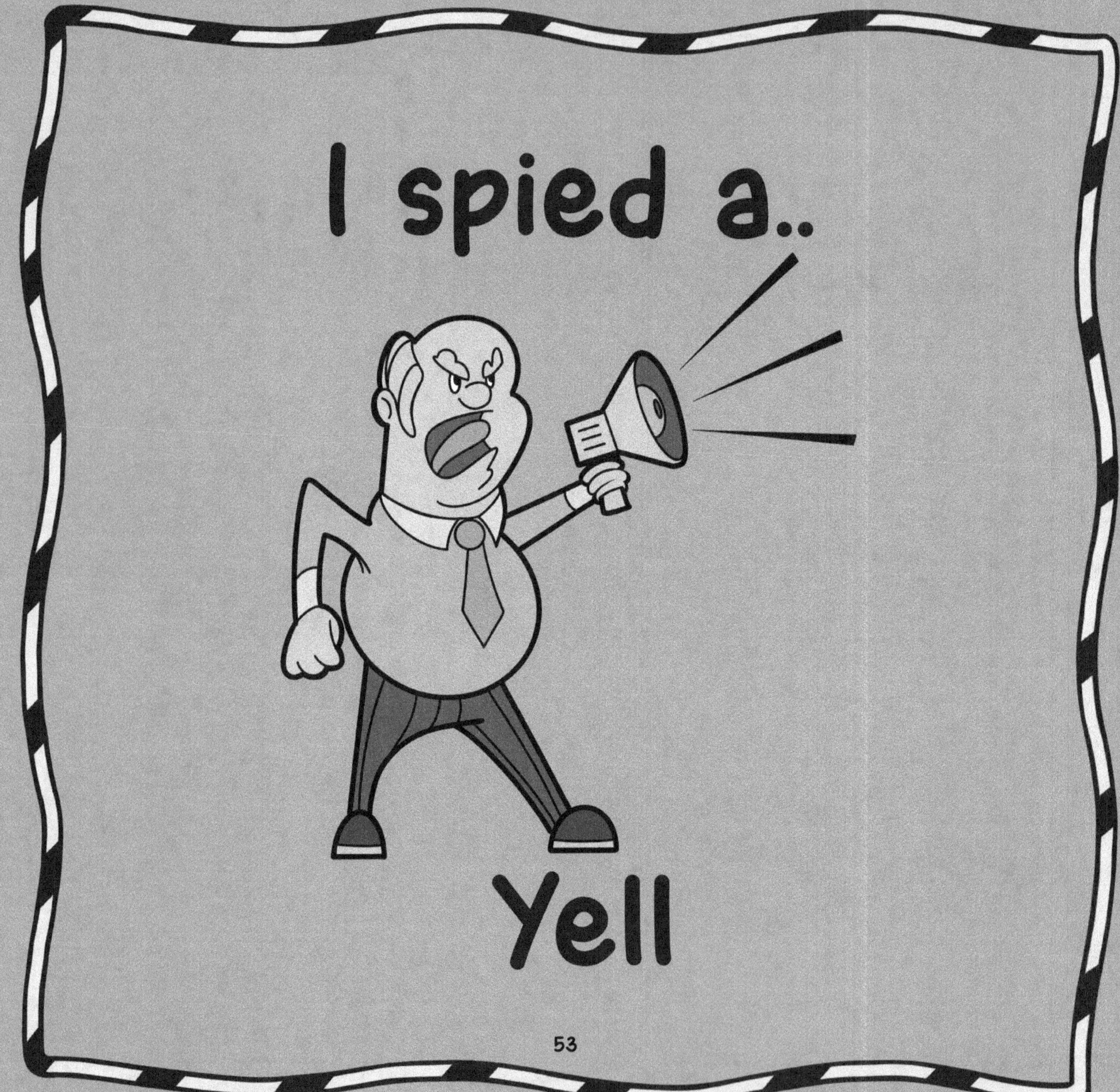

I spied a..
Yell

I Spy With My Little Eye Something Beginning With ...

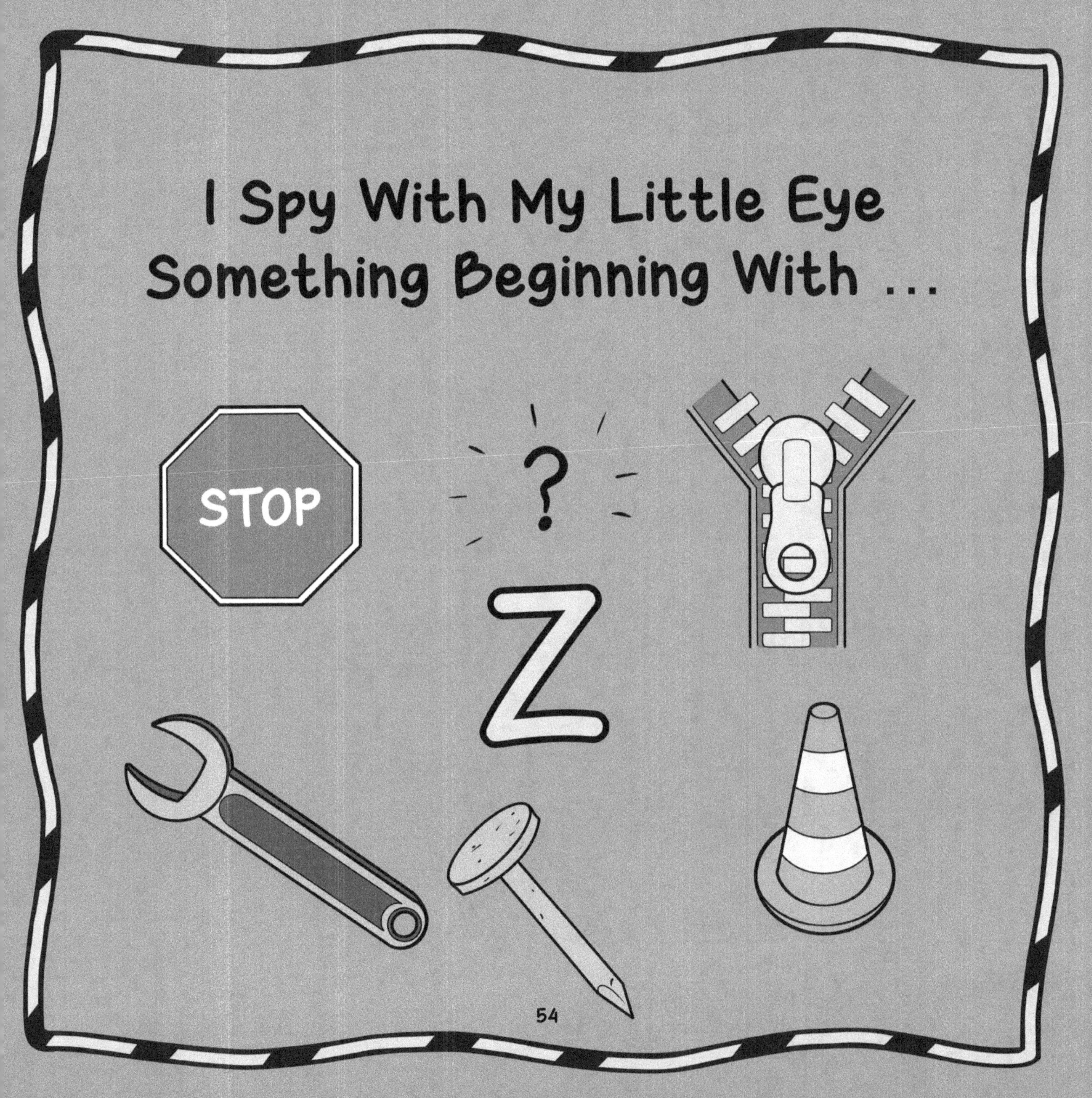

I spied a..

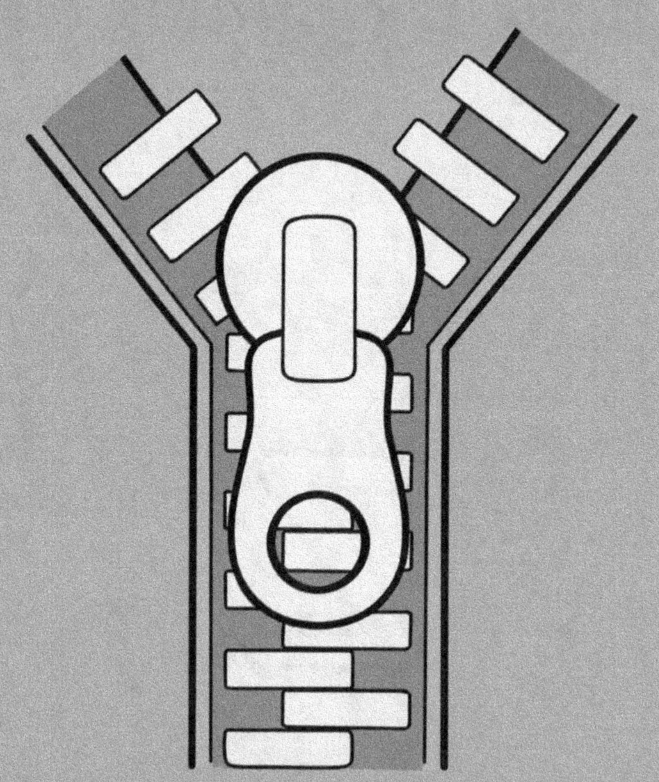

Zip